PYGMALION

George Bernard Shaw

Prestwick House
LITERARY TOUCHSTONE CLASSICS™

P.O. Box 658 Clayton, Delaware 19938 • www.prestwickhouse.com

SENIOR EDITOR: Paul Moliken

EDITORS: Sondra Y. Abel and Lindsay Conley

DESIGN: Wendy Smith

PRODUCTION: Jerry Clark

Prestwick House
LITERARY TOUCHSTONE CLASSICS™

P.O. BOX 658 • CLAYTON, DELAWARE 19938
TEL: 1.800.932.4593
FAX: 1.888.718.9333
WEB: www.prestwickhouse.com

Prestwick House Teaching Units™, Activity Packs™, and Response Journals™ are the perfect complement for these editions. To purchase teaching resources for this book, visit www.prestwickhouse.com

This Prestwick House edition is an unabridged republication, with slight modifications, of *Pygmalion,* published in 1916, by Brentano's, New York.

ISBN 978-1-58049-399-4

PYGMALION

GEORGE BERNARD SHAW

CONTENTS

NOTES

What is a literary classic and why are these classic works important to the world?

A literary classic is a work of the highest excellence that has something important to say about life and/or the human condition and says it with great artistry. A classic, through its enduring presence, has withstood the test of time and is not bound by time, place, or customs. It speaks to us today as forcefully as it spoke to people one hundred or more years ago, and as forcefully as it will speak to people of future generations. For this reason, a classic is said to have universality.

George Bernard Shaw was born in Dublin in 1856 to a lower middle-class family. In his early twenties, he moved to London, England, where he began his career as a writer, speaker, and critic. Before his death following a fall in 1950, he had also become a famous socialist and vegetarian, a feminist and anti-war activist, and an international celebrity.

Shaw's fierce opposition to World War I turned many of his fellow citizens against him, but the outcry was muted by their love for his plays; and before long, the public embraced Shaw as a national treasure. With his reputation ensured, Shaw traveled the world, always speaking out against what he believed was wrong. He stayed for a while in the Soviet Union at Stalin's invitation, but he visited the United States only briefly.

During his life, Shaw wrote more than sixty plays, including *Arms and the Man* (1894), *Man and Superman* (1903), *Pygmalion* (1912), and *Saint Joan* (1923). In addition to his many other accomplishments, George Bernard Shaw earned the Nobel Prize for Literature in 1925.

The fact that a Shaw play is in production somewhere in the world on any given day reflects the popularity of this playwright, whom some critics consider second only to Shakespeare.

READING POINTERS

Reading Pointers for Sharper Insights

As you read through *Pygmalion*, consider the following points:

1. The English language:

   - Does language determine one's status?
   - Should "The Queen's English" be the only proper way of speaking?
   - Are Eliza's syntax and pronunciation actually incorrect, or does Higgins place too much of an emphasis on them?
   - Is Higgins's method of teaching pronunciation compromised by his expectations about Eliza?

2. Gender and class roles in Victorian England were rigidly defined. Audiences were not used to seeing these values questioned. Shaw, though, examined and rejected the idea of each person being trapped in his or her role. Toward the end of the play, Eliza claims that "the difference between a lady and a flower girl is not how she behaves, but how she's treated."

3. The concept that appearance differs from reality is another of Shaw's targets. Although Eliza is the same person from the beginning of the play until the end, Freddie ignores her when she is a lowly flower seller and yet is completely enraptured by her when he views her as a member of high society.

4. What does Eliza actually learn and accomplish? Readers should be aware that the most important change she undergoes is one of self-realization. She learns that accent, vocabulary, and pronunciation are not the measure of a human being; by the end of the play, Eliza is aware that she can function independently of Higgins.

5.   *Pygmalion* is modeled after the Greek myth of Pygmalion and Galatea. Shaw did not, however, restrict himself to simply modernizing the plot. The following elements of the myth are similar to parts of the play, although they are merely points on which Shaw hung the story of Henry Higgins and Eliza Doolittle:

   - Pygmalion, a young sculptor in Cyprus, hates women and resolves never to marry.
   - The sculptor, however, creates a beautiful female statue, with which he falls deeply in love.
   - Because the statue is the perfection of the female form, he dresses it in fine clothing and jewelry.
   - Pygmalion prays to Aphrodite to bring the statue to life, and she does.
   - Galatea (the now-alive statue) and Pygmalion marry.

6.   The contrast between the ending Shaw wrote and readers' expectations of a happy ending (or, at least, a resolution) is explained in his own comments after the conclusion of the play. He claims that the "rest of the story need not be shown" and criticizes readers who lack imaginations. (Henry and Eliza do end up together in "My Fair Lady," the musical based on the play.)

PREFACE

A Professor of Phonetics.

As will be seen later on, Pygmalion needs, not a preface, but a sequel, which I have supplied in its due place.

The English have no respect for their language, and will not teach their children to speak it. They spell it so abominably that no man can teach himself what it sounds like. It is impossible for an Englishman to open his mouth without making some other Englishman hate or despise him. German and Spanish are accessible to foreigners: English is not accessible even to Englishmen. The reformer England needs today is an energetic phonetic enthusiast: that is why I have made such a one the hero of a popular play. There have been heroes of that kind crying in the wilderness for many years past. When I became interested in the subject towards the end of the eighteen-seventies, Melville Bell† was dead; but Alexander J. Ellis† was still a living patriarch, with an impressive head always covered by a velvet skull cap, for which he would apologize to public meetings in a very courtly manner. He and Tito Pagliardini, another phonetic veteran, were men whom it was impossible to dislike. Henry Sweet,† then a young man, lacked their sweetness of character: he was about as conciliatory to conventional mortals as Ibsen† or Samuel Butler.† His great ability as a phonetician (he was, I think, the best of them all at his job) would have entitled him to high official recognition, and perhaps enabled him to

†Terms marked in the text with (†) can be looked up in the Glossary for additional information.

popularize his subject, but for his Satanic contempt for all academic dig-
nitaries and persons in general who thought more of Greek than of phonetics. Once, in the days when the Imperial Institute† rose in South Kensington, and Joseph Chamberlain† was booming the Empire, I induced the
editor of a leading monthly review to commission an article from Sweet
on the imperial importance of his subject. When it arrived, it contained
nothing but a savagely derisive attack on a professor of language and literature whose chair Sweet regarded as proper to a phonetic expert only.
The article, being libelous, had to be returned as impossible; and I had to
renounce my dream of dragging its author into the limelight. When I met
him afterwards, for the first time for many years, I found to my astonish-
ment that he, who had been a quite tolerably presentable young man, had
actually managed by sheer scorn to alter his personal appearance until he
had become a sort of walking repudiation of Oxford† and all its traditions.
It must have been largely in his own despite that he was squeezed into
something called a Readership of phonetics there. The future of phonetics
rests probably with his pupils, who all swore by him; but nothing could
bring the man himself into any sort of compliance with the university, to
which he nevertheless clung by divine right in an intensely Oxonian way. I
daresay his papers, if he has left any, include some satires that may be published without too destructive results fifty years hence. He was, I believe,
not in the least an ill-natured man: very much the opposite, I should say;
but he would not suffer fools gladly.

Those who knew him will recognize in my third act the allusion to
the patent shorthand in which he used to write postcards, and which may
be acquired from a four and six-penny manual published by the Claren-
don Press. The postcards which Mrs. Higgins describes are such as I have
received from Sweet. I would decipher a sound which a cockney would
represent by *zerr*, and a Frenchman by *seu*, and then write demanding
with some heat what on earth it meant. Sweet, with boundless contempt
for my stupidity, would reply that it not only meant but obviously was the
word Result, as no other word containing that sound, and capable of making sense with the context, existed in any language spoken on earth. That
less expert mortals should require fuller indications was beyond Sweet's
patience. Therefore, though the whole point of his "Current Shorthand" is
that it can express every sound in the language perfectly, vowels as well as
consonants, and that your hand has to make no stroke except the easy and
current ones with which you write m, n, and u, l, p, and q, scribbling them
at whatever angle comes easiest to you, his unfortunate determination to

make this remarkable and quite legible script serve also as a shorthand reduced it in his own practice to the most inscrutable of cryptograms. His true objective was the provision of a full, accurate, legible script for our noble but ill-dressed language; but he was led past that by his contempt for the popular Pitman system of shorthand,[†] which he called the Pitfall system. The triumph of Pitman was a triumph of business organization: there was a weekly paper to persuade you to learn Pitman: there were cheap textbooks and exercise books and transcripts of speeches for you to copy, and schools where experienced teachers coached you up to the necessary proficiency. Sweet could not organize his market in that fashion. He might as well have been the Sybil[†] who tore up the leaves of prophecy that nobody would attend to. The four and six-penny manual, mostly in his lithographed handwriting, that was never vulgarly advertized, may perhaps some day be taken up by a syndicate and pushed upon the public as The Times[†] pushed the Encyclopaedia Britannica; but until then it will certainly not prevail against Pitman. I have bought three copies of it during my lifetime; and I am informed by the publishers that its cloistered existence is still a steady and healthy one. I actually learned the system two several times; and yet the shorthand in which I am writing these lines is Pitman's. And the reason is, that my secretary cannot transcribe Sweet, having been perforce taught in the schools of Pitman. Therefore, Sweet railed at Pitman as vainly as Thersites railed at Ajax:[†] his raillery, however it may have eased his soul, gave no popular vogue to Current Shorthand.

Pygmalion[†] Higgins is not a portrait of Sweet, to whom the adventure of Eliza Doolittle would have been impossible; still, as will be seen, there are touches of Sweet in the play. With Higgins's physique and temperament Sweet might have set the Thames[†] on fire. As it was, he impressed himself professionally on Europe to an extent that made his comparative personal obscurity, and the failure of Oxford to do justice to his eminence, a puzzle to foreign specialists in his subject. I do not blame Oxford, because I think Oxford is quite right in demanding a certain social amenity from its nurslings (heaven knows it is not exorbitant in its requirements!); for although I well know how hard it is for a man of genius with a seriously underrated subject to maintain serene and kindly relations with the men who underrate it, and who keep all the best places for less important subjects which they profess without originality and sometimes without much capacity for them, still, if he overwhelms them with wrath and disdain, he cannot expect them to heap honors on him.

Of the later generations of phoneticians I know little. Among them towers the Poet Laureate,[†] to whom perhaps Higgins may owe his Miltonic[†] sympathies, though here again I must disclaim all portraiture. But if the play makes the public aware that there are such people as phoneticians, and that they are among the most important people in England at present, it will serve its turn.

I wish to boast that Pygmalion has been an extremely successful play all over Europe and North America as well as at home. It is so intensely and deliberately didactic, and its subject is esteemed so dry, that I delight in throwing it at the heads of the wiseacres who repeat the parrot cry that art should never be didactic. It goes to prove my contention that art should never be anything else.

Finally, and for the encouragement of people troubled with accents that cut them off from all high employment, I may add that the change wrought by Professor Higgins in the flower girl is neither impossible nor uncommon. The modern concierge's daughter who fulfils her ambition by playing the Queen of Spain in Ruy Blas at the Théâtre Francais is only one of many thousands of men and women who have sloughed off their native dialects and acquired a new tongue. But the thing has to be done scientifically, or the last state of the aspirant may be worse than the first. An honest and natural slum dialect is more tolerable than the attempt of a phonetically untaught person to imitate the vulgar dialect of the golf club; and I am sorry to say that in spite of the efforts of our Academy of Dramatic Art,[†] there is still too much sham golfing English on our stage, and too little of the noble English of Forbes Robertson.

Act I

[Covent Garden at 11.15 p.m. Torrents of heavy summer rain. Cab whistles blowing frantically in all directions. Pedestrians running for shelter into the market and under the portico of St. Paul's Church, where there are already several people, among them a lady and her daughter in evening dress. They are all peering out gloomily at the rain, except one man with his back turned to the rest, who seems wholly preoccupied with a notebook in which he is writing busily.

The church clock strikes the first quarter.]

THE DAUGHTER: *[in the space between the central pillars, close to the one on her left]* I'm getting chilled to the bone. What can Freddy be doing all this time? He's been gone twenty minutes.

THE MOTHER: *[on her daughter's right]* Not so long. But he ought to have got us a cab by this.

A BYSTANDER: *[on the lady's right]* He won't get no cab not until half-past eleven, missus, when they come back after dropping their theatre fares.

THE MOTHER: But we must have a cab. We can't stand here until half-past eleven. It's too bad.

THE BYSTANDER: Well, it ain't my fault, missus.

THE DAUGHTER: If Freddy had a bit of gumption, he would have got one at the theatre door.

THE MOTHER: What could he have done, poor boy?

15

THE DAUGHTER: Other people got cabs. Why couldn't he?

[Freddy rushes in out of the rain from the Southampton Street side, and comes between them closing a dripping umbrella. He is a young man of twenty, in evening dress, very wet around the ankles.]

THE DAUGHTER: Well, haven't you got a cab?

FREDDY: There's not one to be had for love or money.

THE MOTHER: Oh, Freddy, there must be one. You can't have tried.

THE DAUGHTER: It's too tiresome. Do you expect us to go and get one ourselves?

FREDDY: I tell you they're all engaged. The rain was so sudden: nobody was prepared; and everybody had to take a cab. I've been to Charing Cross one way and nearly to Ludgate Circus the other; and they were all engaged.

THE MOTHER: Did you try Trafalgar Square?

FREDDY: There wasn't one at Trafalgar Square.

THE DAUGHTER: Did you try?

FREDDY: I tried as far as Charing Cross Station. Did you expect me to walk to Hammersmith?

THE DAUGHTER: You haven't tried at all.

THE MOTHER: You really are very helpless, Freddy. Go again; and don't come back until you have found a cab.

FREDDY: I shall simply get soaked for nothing.

THE DAUGHTER: And what about us? Are we to stay here all night in this draught, with next to nothing on. You selfish pig—

FREDDY: Oh, very well: I'll go, I'll go. *[He opens his umbrella and dashes off Strandwards, but comes into collision with a flower girl, who is hurrying in for shelter, knocking her basket out of her hands. A blinding flash of lightning, followed instantly by a rattling peal of thunder, orchestrates the incident]*

THE FLOWER GIRL: Nah then, Freddy: look wh' y' gowin, deah.

FREDDY: Sorry *[he rushes off]*.

THE FLOWER GIRL: *[picking up her scattered flowers and replacing them in the basket]* There's menners f' yer! Te-oo banches o voylets trod into the mad. *[She sits down on the plinth of the column, sorting her flowers, on the lady's right. She is not at all an attractive person. She is perhaps eighteen, perhaps twenty, hardly older. She wears a little sailor hat of black straw that has long been exposed to the dust and soot of London and has seldom if ever been*

*brushed. Her hair needs washing rather badly: its mousy color can hardly be
natural. She wears a shoddy black coat that reaches nearly to her knees and is
shaped to her waist. She has a brown skirt with a coarse apron. Her boots are
much the worse for wear. She is no doubt as clean as she can afford to be; but
compared to the ladies she is very dirty. Her features are no worse than theirs;
but their condition leaves something to be desired; and she needs the services
of a dentist].*

THE MOTHER: How do you know that my son's name is Freddy, pray?

THE FLOWER GIRL: Ow, eez ye-ooa san, is e? Wal, fewd dan y' de-ooty baw-
mz a mather should, eed now bettern to spawl a pore gel's flahrzn than
ran awy athaht pyin. Will ye-oo py me f'them? *[Here, with apologies, this
desperate attempt to represent her dialect without a phonetic alphabet must be
abandoned as unintelligible outside London.]*

THE DAUGHTER: Do nothing of the sort, mother. The idea!

THE MOTHER: Please allow me, Clara. Have you any pennies?

THE DAUGHTER: No. I've nothing smaller than sixpence.

THE FLOWER GIRL: *[hopefully]* I can give you change for a tanner, kind lady.

THE MOTHER: *[to Clara]* Give it to me. *[Clara parts reluctantly]*. Now *[to the
girl]* this is for your flowers.

THE FLOWER GIRL: Thank you kindly, lady.

THE DAUGHTER: Make her give you the change. These things are only a
penny a bunch.

THE MOTHER: Do hold your tongue, Clara. *[To the girl]*. You can keep the
change.

THE FLOWER GIRL: Oh, thank you, lady.

THE MOTHER: Now tell me how you know that young gentleman's name.

THE FLOWER GIRL: I didn't.

THE MOTHER: I heard you call him by it. Don't try to deceive me.

THE FLOWER GIRL: *[protesting]* Who's trying to deceive you? I called him
Freddy or Charlie same as you might yourself if you was talking to a
stranger and wished to be pleasant. *[She sits down beside her basket]*.

THE DAUGHTER: Sixpence thrown away! Really, mamma, you might have
spared Freddy that. *[She retreats in disgust behind the pillar]*.

*[An elderly gentleman of the amiable military type rushes into shelter, and closes a
dripping umbrella. He is in the same plight as Freddy, very wet about the ankles.
He is in evening dress, with a light overcoat. He takes the place left vacant by the
daughter's retirement.]*

THE GENTLEMAN: Phew!

THE MOTHER: *[to the gentleman]* Oh, sir, is there any sign of its stopping?

THE GENTLEMAN: I'm afraid not. It started worse than ever about two minutes ago. *[He goes to the plinth beside the flower girl; puts up his foot on it; and stoops to turn down his trouser ends]*.

THE MOTHER: Oh, dear! *[She retires sadly and joins her daughter]*.

THE FLOWER GIRL: *[taking advantage of the military gentleman's proximity to establish friendly relations with him]*. If it's worse it's a sign it's nearly over. So cheer up, Captain; and buy a flower off a poor girl.

THE GENTLEMAN: I'm sorry, I haven't any change.

THE FLOWER GIRL: I can give you change, Captain.

THE GENTLEMAN: For a sovereign? I've nothing less.

THE FLOWER GIRL: Garn! Oh do buy a flower off me, Captain. I can change half-a-crown. Take this for tuppence.

THE GENTLEMAN: Now don't be troublesome: there's a good girl. *[Trying his pockets]* I really haven't any change—Stop: here's three hapence, if that's any use to you *[he retreats to the other pillar]*.

THE FLOWER GIRL: *[disappointed, but thinking three halfpence better than nothing]* Thank you, sir.

THE BYSTANDER: *[to the girl]* You be careful: give him a flower for it. There's a bloke here behind taking down every blessed word you're saying. *[All turn to the man who is taking notes]*.

THE FLOWER GIRL: *[springing up terrified]* I ain't done nothing wrong by speaking to the gentleman. I've a right to sell flowers if I keep off the kerb. *[Hysterically]* I'm a respectable girl: so help me, I never spoke to him except to ask him to buy a flower off me. *[General hubbub, mostly sympathetic to the flower girl, but deprecating her excessive sensibility. Cries of* Don't start hollerin. Who's hurting you? Nobody's going to touch you. What's the good of fussing? Steady on. Easy, easy, etc., *come from the elderly staid spectators, who pat her comfortingly. Less patient ones bid her shut her head, or ask her roughly what is wrong with her. A remoter group, not knowing what the matter is, crowd in and increase the noise with question and answer:* What's the row? What she do? Where is he? A tec taking her down. What! him? Yes: him over there: Took money off the gentleman, etc. *The flower girl, distraught and mobbed, breaks through them to the gentleman, crying mildly]* Oh, sir, don't let him charge me. You dunno what it means to me. They'll take away my character and drive me on the streets for speaking to gentlemen. They—

THE NOTE TAKER: *[coming forward on her right, the rest crowding after him]* There, there, there, there! Who's hurting you, you silly girl? What do you take me for?

THE BYSTANDER: It's all right: he's a gentleman: look at his boots. *[Explaining to the note taker]* She thought you was a copper's nark, sir.

THE NOTE TAKER: *[with quick interest]* What's a copper's nark?

THE BYSTANDER: *[inept at definition]* It's a—well, it's a copper's nark, as you might say. What else would you call it? A sort of informer.

THE FLOWER GIRL: *[still hysterical]* I take my Bible oath I never said a word—

THE NOTE TAKER: *[overbearing but good-humored]* Oh, shut up, shut up. Do I look like a policeman?

THE FLOWER GIRL: *[far from reassured]* Then what did you take down my words for? How do I know whether you took me down right? You just show me what you've wrote about me. *[The note taker opens his book and holds it steadily under her nose, though the pressure of the mob trying to read it over his shoulders would upset a weaker man]*. What's that? That ain't proper writing. I can't read that.

THE NOTE TAKER: I can. *[Reads, reproducing her pronunciation exactly]* "Cheer ap, Keptin; n' haw ya flahr orf a pore gel."

THE FLOWER GIRL: *[much distressed]* It's because I called him Captain. I meant no harm. *[To the gentleman]* Oh, sir, don't let him lay a charge agen me for a word like that. You—

THE GENTLEMAN: Charge! I make no charge. *[To the note taker]* Really, sir, if you are a detective, you need not begin protecting me against molestation by young women until I ask you. Anybody could see that the girl meant no harm.

THE BYSTANDERS GENERALLY: *[demonstrating against police espionage]* Course they could. What business is it of yours? You mind your own affairs. He wants promotion, he does. Taking down people's words! Girl never said a word to him. What harm if she did? Nice thing a girl can't shelter from the rain without being insulted, etc., etc., etc. *[She is conducted by the more sympathetic demonstrators back to her plinth, where she resumes her seat and struggles with her emotion]*.

THE BYSTANDER: He ain't a tec. He's a blooming busybody: that's what he is. I tell you, look at his boots.

THE NOTE TAKER: *[turning on him genially]* And how are all your people down at Selsey?

THE BYSTANDER: *[suspiciously]* Who told you my people come from Selsey?

THE NOTE TAKER: Never you mind. They did. *[To the girl]* How do you come to be up so far east? You were born in Lisson Grove.

THE FLOWER GIRL: *[appalled]* Oh, what harm is there in my leaving Lisson Grove? It wasn't fit for a pig to live in; and I had to pay four-and-six a week. *[In tears]* Oh, boo—hoo—oo—

THE NOTE TAKER: Live where you like; but stop that noise.

THE GENTLEMAN: *[to the girl]* Come, come! he can't touch you: you have a right to live where you please.

A SARCASTIC BYSTANDER: *[thrusting himself between the note taker and the gentleman]* Park Lane, for instance. I'd like to go into the Housing Question with you, I would.

THE FLOWER GIRL: *[subsiding into a brooding melancholy over her basket, and talking very low-spiritedly to herself]* I'm a good girl, I am.

THE SARCASTIC BYSTANDER: *[not attending to her]* Do you know where I come from?

THE NOTE TAKER: *[promptly]* Hoxton.

[Titterings. Popular interest in the note taker's performance increases.]

THE SARCASTIC ONE: *[amazed]* Well, who said I didn't? Bly me! You know everything, you do.

THE FLOWER GIRL: *[still nursing her sense of injury]* Ain't no call to meddle with me, he ain't.

THE BYSTANDER: *[to her]* Of course he ain't. Don't you stand it from him. *[To the note taker]* See here: what call have you to know about people what never offered to meddle with you? Where's your warrant?

SEVERAL BYSTANDERS: *[encouraged by this seeming point of law]* Yes: where's your warrant?

THE FLOWER GIRL: Let him say what he likes. I don't want to have no truck with him.

THE BYSTANDER: You take us for dirt under your feet, don't you? Catch you taking liberties with a gentleman!

THE SARCASTIC BYSTANDER: Yes: tell him where he come from if you want to go fortune-telling.

THE NOTE TAKER: Cheltenham, Harrow, Cambridge, and India.

THE GENTLEMAN: Quite right. *[Great laughter. Reaction in the note taker's favor. Exclamations of He knows all about it. Told him proper. Hear him tell the toff where he come from? etc.].* May I ask, sir, do you do this for your living at a music hall?

THE NOTE TAKER: I've thought of that. Perhaps I shall some day.

[The rain has stopped; and the persons on the outside of the crowd begin to drop off.]

THE FLOWER GIRL: *[resenting the reaction]* He's no gentleman, he ain't, to interfere with a poor girl.

THE DAUGHTER: *[out of patience, pushing her way rudely to the front and displacing the gentleman, who politely retires to the other side of the pillar]* What on earth is Freddy doing? I shall get pneumonia if I stay in this draught any longer.

THE NOTE TAKER: *[to himself, hastily making a note of her pronunciation of "monia"]* Earlscourt.

THE DAUGHTER: *[violently]* Will you please keep your impertinent remarks to yourself?

THE NOTE TAKER: Did I say that out loud? I didn't mean to. I beg your pardon. Your mother's Epsom, unmistakeably.

THE MOTHER: *[advancing between her daughter and the note taker]* How very curious! I was brought up in Largelady Park, near Epsom.

THE NOTE TAKER: *[uproariously amused]* Ha! ha! What a devil of a name! Excuse me. *[To the daughter]* You want a cab, do you?

THE DAUGHTER: Don't dare speak to me.

THE MOTHER: Oh, please, please Clara. *[Her daughter repudiates her with an angry shrug and retires haughtily.]* We should be so grateful to you, sir, if you found us a cab. *[The note taker produces a whistle]*. Oh, thank you. *[She joins her daughter]*.

[The note taker blows a piercing blast.]

THE SARCASTIC BYSTANDER: There! I knowed he was a plain-clothes copper.

THE BYSTANDER: That ain't a police whistle: that's a sporting whistle.

THE FLOWER GIRL: *[still preoccupied with her wounded feelings]* He's no right to take away my character. My character is the same to me as any lady's.

THE NOTE TAKER: I don't know whether you've noticed it; but the rain stopped about two minutes ago.

THE BYSTANDER: So it has. Why didn't you say so before? and us losing our time listening to your silliness. *[He walks off towards the Strand]*.

THE SARCASTIC BYSTANDER: I can tell where you come from. You come from Anwell. Go back there.

THE NOTE TAKER: *[helpfully]* Hanwell.

THE SARCASTIC BYSTANDER: *[affecting great distinction of speech]* Thenk you, teacher. Haw haw! So long *[he touches his hat with mock respect and strolls off]*.

THE FLOWER GIRL: Frightening people like that! How would he like it himself.

THE MOTHER: It's quite fine now, Clara. We can walk to a motor bus. Come. *[She gathers her skirts above her ankles and hurries off towards the Strand]*.

THE DAUGHTER: But the cab—*[her mother is out of hearing]*. Oh, how tiresome! *[She follows angrily]*.

[All the rest have gone except the note taker, the gentleman, and the flower girl, who sits arranging her basket, and still pitying herself in murmurs.]

THE FLOWER GIRL: Poor girl! Hard enough for her to live without being worrited and chivied.

THE GENTLEMAN: *[returning to his former place on the note taker's left]* How do you do it, if I may ask?

THE NOTE TAKER: Simply phonetics. The science of speech. That's my profession; also my hobby. Happy is the man who can make a living by his hobby! You can spot an Irishman or a Yorkshireman by his brogue. I can place any man within six miles. I can place him within two miles in London. Sometimes within two streets.

THE FLOWER GIRL: Ought to be ashamed of himself, unmanly coward!

THE GENTLEMAN: But is there a living in that?

THE NOTE TAKER: Oh yes. Quite a fat one. This is an age of upstarts. Men begin in Kentish Town with 80 pounds a year, and end in Park Lane with a hundred thousand. They want to drop Kentish Town; but they give themselves away every time they open their mouths. Now I can teach them—

THE FLOWER GIRL: Let him mind his own business and leave a poor girl—

THE NOTE TAKER: *[explosively]* Woman: cease this detestable boohooing instantly; or else seek the shelter of some other place of worship.

THE FLOWER GIRL: *[with feeble defiance]* I've a right to be here if I like, same as you.

THE NOTE TAKER: A woman who utters such depressing and disgusting sounds has no right to be anywhere—no right to live. Remember that you are a human being with a soul and the divine gift of articulate speech: that your native language is the language of Shakespear and Milton and The Bible; and don't sit there crooning like a bilious pigeon.

THE FLOWER GIRL: [*quite overwhelmed, and looking up at him in mingled wonder and deprecation without daring to raise her head*] Ah—ah—ah—ow—ow—oo!

THE NOTE TAKER: [*whipping out his book*] Heavens! what a sound! [*He writes; then holds out the book and reads, reproducing her vowels exactly*] Ah—ah—ah—ow—ow—ow—oo!

THE FLOWER GIRL: [*tickled by the performance, and laughing in spite of herself*] Garn!

THE NOTE TAKER: You see this creature with her kerbstone English: the English that will keep her in the gutter to the end of her days. Well, sir, in three months I could pass that girl off as a duchess at an ambassador's garden party. I could even get her a place as lady's maid or shop assistant, which requires better English. That's the sort of thing I do for commercial millionaires. And on the profits of it I do genuine scientific work in phonetics, and a little as a poet on Miltonic lines.

THE GENTLEMAN: I am myself a student of Indian dialects; and—

THE NOTE TAKER: [*eagerly*] Are you? Do you know Colonel Pickering, the author of Spoken Sanscrit?†

THE GENTLEMAN: I am Colonel Pickering. Who are you?

THE NOTE TAKER: Henry Higgins, author of Higgins's Universal Alphabet.

PICKERING: [*with enthusiasm*] I came from India to meet you.

HIGGINS: I was going to India to meet you.

PICKERING: Where do you live?

HIGGINS: 27A Wimpole Street. Come and see me tomorrow.

PICKERING: I'm at the Carlton. Come with me now and let's have a jaw over† some supper.

HIGGINS: Right you are.

THE FLOWER GIRL: [*to Pickering, as he passes her*] Buy a flower, kind gentleman. I'm short for my lodging.

PICKERING: I really haven't any change. I'm sorry [*he goes away*].

HIGGINS: [*shocked at girl's mendacity*] Liar. You said you could change half-a-crown.

THE FLOWER GIRL: [*rising in desperation*] You ought to be stuffed with nails, you ought. [*Flinging the basket at his feet*] Take the whole blooming basket for sixpence.

[The church clock strikes the second quarter.]

HIGGINS: *[hearing in it the voice of God, rebuking him for his Pharisaic want of charity† to the poor girl]* A reminder. *[He raises his hat solemnly; then throws a handful of money into the basket and follows Pickering].*

THE FLOWER GIRL: *[picking up a half-crown]* Ah—ow—ooh! *[Picking up a couple of florins]* Aaah—ow—ooh! *[Picking up several coins]* Aaaaaah—ow—ooh! *[Picking up a half-sovereign]* Aaaaaaaaaaaah—ow—ooh!!!

FREDDY: *[springing out of a taxicab]* Got one at last. Hallo! *[To the girl]* Where are the two ladies that were here?

THE FLOWER GIRL: They walked to the bus when the rain stopped.

FREDDY: And left me with a cab on my hands. Damnation!

THE FLOWER GIRL: *[with grandeur]* Never you mind, young man. I'm going home in a taxi. *[She sails off to the cab. The driver puts his hand behind him and holds the door firmly shut against her. Quite understanding his mistrust, she shows him her handful of money].* Eightpence ain't no object to me, Charlie. *[He grins and opens the door].* Angel Court, Drury Lane, round the corner of Micklejohn's oil shop. Let's see how fast you can make her hop it. *[She gets in and pulls the door to with a slam as the taxicab starts].*

FREDDY: Well, I'm dashed!

ACT II

[Next day at 11 a.m. Higgins's laboratory in Wimpole Street. It is a room on the first floor, looking on the street, and was meant for the drawing-room. The double doors are in the middle of the back wall; and persons entering find in the corner to their right two tall file cabinets at right angles to one another against the walls. In this corner stands a flat writing-table, on which are a phonograph, a laryngoscope, a row of tiny organ pipes with a bellows, a set of lamp chimneys for singing flames with burners attached to a gas plug in the wall by an indiarubber tube, several tuning-forks of different sizes, a life-size image of half a human head, showing in section the vocal organs, and a box containing a supply of wax cylinders for the phonograph.

Further down the room, on the same side, is a fireplace, with a comfortable leather-covered easy-chair at the side of the hearth nearest the door, and a coal-scuttle. There is a clock on the mantelpiece. Between the fireplace and the phonograph table is a stand for newspapers.

On the other side of the central door, to the left of the visitor, is a cabinet of shallow drawers. On it is a telephone and the telephone directory. The corner beyond, and most of the side wall, is occupied by a grand piano, with the keyboard at the end furthest from the door, and a bench for the player extending the full length of the keyboard. On the piano is a dessert dish heaped with fruit and sweets, mostly chocolates.

The middle of the room is clear. Besides the easy chair, the piano bench, and two chairs at the phonograph table, there is one stray chair. It stands near the fireplace. On the walls, engravings; mostly Piranesis[†] and mezzotint portraits.[†] No paintings.

Pickering is seated at the table, putting down some cards and a tuning-fork which he has been using. Higgins is standing up near him, closing two or three file drawers which are hanging out. He appears in the morning light as a robust, vital, appetizing sort of man of forty or thereabouts, dressed in a professional-looking black frock-coat with a white linen collar and black silk tie. He is of the energetic, scientific type, heartily, even violently interested in everything that can be studied as a scientific subject, and careless about himself and other people, including their feelings. He is, in fact, but for his years and size, rather like a very impetuous baby "taking notice" eagerly and loudly, and requiring almost as much watching to keep him out of unintended mischief. His manner varies from genial bullying when he is in a good humor to stormy petulance when anything goes wrong; but he is so entirely frank and void of malice that he remains likeable even in his least reasonable moments.]

HIGGINS: *[as he shuts the last drawer]* Well, I think that's the whole show.

PICKERING: It's really amazing. I haven't taken half of it in, you know.

HIGGINS: Would you like to go over any of it again?

PICKERING: *[rising and coming to the fireplace, where he plants himself with his back to the fire]* No, thank you; not now. I'm quite done up for this morning.

HIGGINS: *[following him, and standing beside him on his left]* Tired of listening to sounds?

PICKERING: Yes. It's a fearful strain. I rather fancied myself because I can pronounce twenty-four distinct vowel sounds; but your hundred and thirty beat me. I can't hear a bit of difference between most of them.

HIGGINS: *[chuckling, and going over to the piano to eat sweets]* Oh, that comes with practice. You hear no difference at first; but you keep on listening, and presently you find they're all as different as A from B. *[Mrs. Pearce looks in: she is Higgins's housekeeper]* What's the matter?

MRS. PEARCE: *[hesitating, evidently perplexed]* A young woman wants to see you, sir.

HIGGINS: A young woman! What does she want?

MRS. PEARCE: Well, sir, she says you'll be glad to see her when you know what she's come about. She's quite a common girl, sir. Very common indeed. I should have sent her away, only I thought perhaps you wanted her to talk into your machines. I hope I've not done wrong; but really you see such queer people sometimes—you'll excuse me, I'm sure, sir—

HIGGINS: Oh, that's all right, Mrs. Pearce. Has she an interesting accent?

MRS. PEARCE: Oh, something dreadful, sir, really. I don't know how you can take an interest in it.

HIGGINS: *[to Pickering]* Let's have her up. Show her up, Mrs. Pearce *[he rushes across to his working table and picks out a cylinder to use on the phonograph]*.

MRS. PEARCE: *[only half resigned to it]* Very well, sir. It's for you to say. *[She goes downstairs]*.

HIGGINS: This is rather a bit of luck. I'll show you how I make records. We'll set her talking; and I'll take it down first in Bell's visible Speech; then in broad Romic; and then we'll get her on the phonograph so that you can turn her on as often as you like with the written transcript before you.

MRS. PEARCE: *[returning]* This is the young woman, sir.

[The flower girl enters in state. She has a hat with three ostrich feathers, orange, sky-blue, and red. She has a nearly clean apron, and the shoddy coat has been tidied a little. The pathos of this deplorable figure, with its innocent vanity and consequential air, touches Pickering, who has already straightened himself in the presence of Mrs. Pearce. But as to Higgins, the only distinction he makes between men and women is that when he is neither bullying nor exclaiming to the heavens against some featherweight cross, he coaxes women as a child coaxes its nurse when it wants to get anything out of her.]

HIGGINS: *[brusquely, recognizing her with unconcealed disappointment, and at once, babylike, making an intolerable grievance of it]* Why, this is the girl I jotted down last night. She's no use: I've got all the records I want of the Lisson Grove lingo; and I'm not going to waste another cylinder on it. *[To the girl]* Be off with you: I don't want you.

THE FLOWER GIRL: Don't you be so saucy. You ain't heard what I come for yet. *[To Mrs. Pearce, who is waiting at the door for further instruction]* Did you tell him I come in a taxi?

MRS. PEARCE: Nonsense, girl! what do you think a gentleman like Mr. Higgins cares what you came in?

THE FLOWER GIRL: Oh, we are proud! He ain't above giving lessons, not him: I heard him say so. Well, I ain't come here to ask for any compliment; and if my money's not good enough I can go elsewhere.

HIGGINS: Good enough for what?

The Flower Girl: Good enough for ye—oo. Now you know, don't you? I'm come to have lessons, I am. And to pay for em too: make no mistake.

Higgins:[stupent] WELL!!! [Recovering his breath with a gasp] What do you expect me to say to you?

The Flower Girl: Well, if you was a gentleman, you might ask me to sit down, I think. Don't I tell you I'm bringing you business?

Higgins: Pickering: shall we ask this baggage to sit down or shall we throw her out of the window?

The Flower Girl: [running away in terror to the piano, where she turns at bay] Ah—ah—ah—ow—ow—ow—oo! [Wounded and whimpering] I won't be called a baggage when I've offered to pay like any lady.

[Motionless, the two men stare at her from the other side of the room, amazed.]

Pickering: [gently] What is it you want, my girl?

The Flower Girl: I want to be a lady in a flower shop stead of selling at the corner of Tottenham Court Road. But they won't take me unless I can talk more genteel. He said he could teach me. Well, here I am ready to pay him—not asking any favor—and he treats me as if I was dirt.

Mrs. Pearce: How can you be such a foolish ignorant girl as to think you could afford to pay Mr. Higgins?

The Flower Girl: Why shouldn't I? I know what lessons cost as well as you do; and I'm ready to pay.

Higgins: How much?

The Flower Girl: [coming back to him, triumphant] Now you're talking! I thought you'd come off it when you saw a chance of getting back a bit of what you chucked at me last night. [Confidentially] You'd had a drop in, hadn't you?

Higgins: [peremptorily] Sit down.

The Flower Girl: Oh, if you're going to make a compliment of it—

Higgins: [thundering at her] Sit down.

Mrs. Pearce: [severely] Sit down, girl. Do as you're told. [She places the stray chair near the hearthrug between Higgins and Pickering, and stands behind it waiting for the girl to sit down].

The Flower Girl: Ah—ah—ah—ow—ow—oo! [She stands, half rebellious, half bewildered].

PICKERING: *[very courteous]* Won't you sit down?

LIZA: *[coyly]* Don't mind if I do. *[She sits down. Pickering returns to the hearthrug].*

HIGGINS: What's your name?

THE FLOWER GIRL: Liza Doolittle.

HIGGINS: *[declaiming gravely]*

        Eliza, Elizabeth, Betsy and Bess,

        They went to the woods to get a birds nes':

PICKERING: They found a nest with four eggs in it:

HIGGINS: They took one apiece, and left three in it.

[They laugh heartily at their own wit.]

LIZA: Oh, don't be silly.

MRS. PEARCE: You mustn't speak to the gentleman like that.

LIZA: Well, why won't he speak sensible to me?

HIGGINS: Come back to business. How much do you propose to pay me for the lessons?

LIZA: Oh, I know what's right. A lady friend of mine gets French lessons for eighteenpence an hour from a real French gentleman. Well, you wouldn't have the face to ask me the same for teaching me my own language as you would for French; so I won't give more than a shilling. Take it or leave it.

HIGGINS: *[walking up and down the room, rattling his keys and his cash in his pockets]* You know, Pickering, if you consider a shilling, not as a simple shilling, but as a percentage of this girl's income, it works out as fully equivalent to sixty or seventy guineas from a millionaire.

PICKERING: How so?

HIGGINS: Figure it out. A millionaire has about 150 pounds a day. She earns about half-a-crown.

LIZA: *[haughtily]* Who told you I only—

HIGGINS: *[continuing]* She offers me two-fifths of her day's income for a lesson. Two-fifths of a millionaire's income for a day would be somewhere about 60 pounds. It's handsome. By George, it's enormous! it's the biggest offer I ever had.

LIZA: *[rising, terrified]* Sixty pounds! What are you talking about? I never offered you sixty pounds. Where would I get—

HIGGINS: Hold your tongue.

LIZA: *[weeping]* But I ain't got sixty pounds. Oh—

MRS. PEARCE: Don't cry, you silly girl. Sit down. Nobody is going to touch your money.

HIGGINS: Somebody is going to touch you, with a broomstick, if you don't stop snivelling. Sit down.

LIZA: [obeying slowly] Ah—ah—ah—ow—oo—o! One would think you was my father.

HIGGINS: If I decide to teach you, I'll be worse than two fathers to you. Here! [he offers her his silk handkerchief]

LIZA: What's this for?

HIGGINS: To wipe your eyes. To wipe any part of your face that feels moist. Remember: that's your handkerchief; and that's your sleeve. Don't mistake the one for the other if you wish to become a lady in a shop.

[Liza, utterly bewildered, stares helplessly at him.]

MRS. PEARCE: It's no use talking to her like that, Mr. Higgins: she doesn't understand you. Besides, you're quite wrong: she doesn't do it that way at all [she takes the handkerchief].

LIZA: [snatching it] Here! You give me that handkerchief. He give it to me, not to you.

PICKERING: [laughing] He did. I think it must be regarded as her property, Mrs. Pearce.

MRS. PEARCE: [resigning herself] Serve you right, Mr. Higgins.

PICKERING: Higgins: I'm interested. What about the ambassador's garden party? I'll say you're the greatest teacher alive if you make that good. I'll bet you all the expenses of the experiment you can't do it. And I'll pay for the lessons.

LIZA: Oh, you are real good. Thank you, Captain.

HIGGINS: [tempted, looking at her] It's almost irresistible. She's so deliciously low—so horribly dirty—

LIZA: [protesting extremely] Ah—ah—ah—ah—ow—ow—oooo!!! I ain't dirty: I washed my face and hands afore I come, I did.

PICKERING: You're certainly not going to turn her head with flattery, Higgins.

MRS. PEARCE: [uneasy] Oh, don't say that, sir: there's more ways than one of turning a girl's head; and nobody can do it better than Mr. Higgins, though he may not always mean it. I do hope, sir, you won't encourage him to do anything foolish.

HIGGINS: *[becoming excited as the idea grows on him]* What is life but a series of inspired follies? The difficulty is to find them to do. Never lose a chance: it doesn't come every day. I shall make a duchess of this draggletailed guttersnipe.

LIZA: *[strongly deprecating this view of her]* Ah—ah—ah—ow—ow—oo!

HIGGINS: *[carried away]* Yes: in six months—in three if she has a good ear and a quick tongue—I'll take her anywhere and pass her off as anything. We'll start today: now! this moment! Take her away and clean her, Mrs. Pearce. Monkey Brand, if it won't come off any other way. Is there a good fire in the kitchen?

MRS. PEARCE: *[protesting]*. Yes; but—

HIGGINS:*[storming on]* Take all her clothes off and burn them. Ring up Whiteley or somebody for new ones. Wrap her up in brown paper till they come.

LIZA: You're no gentleman, you're not, to talk of such things. I'm a good girl, I am; and I know what the like of you are, I do.

HIGGINS: We want none of your Lisson Grove prudery here, young woman. You've got to learn to behave like a duchess. Take her away, Mrs. Pearce. If she gives you any trouble wallop her.

LIZA: *[springing up and running between Pickering and Mrs Pearce for protection]* No! I'll call the police, I will.

MRS. PEARCE: But I've no place to put her.

HIGGINS: Put her in the dustbin.

LIZA: Ah—ah—ah—ow—ow—oo!

PICKERING: Oh come, Higgins! be reasonable.

MRS. PEARCE: *[resolutely]* You must be reasonable, Mr. Higgins: really you must. You can't walk over everybody like this.

[Higgins, thus scolded, subsides. The hurricane is succeeded by a zephyr of amiable surprise.]

HIGGINS: *[with professional exquisiteness of modulation]* I walk over everybody! My dear Mrs. Pearce, my dear Pickering, I never had the slightest intention of walking over anyone. All I propose is that we should be kind to this poor girl. We must help her to prepare and fit herself for her new station in life. If I did not express myself clearly it was because I did not wish to hurt her delicacy, or yours.

[Liza, reassured, steals back to her chair.]

MRS. PEARCE: [to Pickering] Well, did you ever hear anything like that, sir?

PICKERING: [laughing heartily] Never, Mrs. Pearce: never.

HIGGINS: [patiently] What's the matter?

MRS. PEARCE: Well, the matter is, sir, that you can't take a girl up like that as if you were picking up a pebble on the beach.

HIGGINS: Why not?

MRS. PEARCE: Why not! But you don't know anything about her. What about her parents? She may be married.

LIZA: Garn!

HIGGINS: There! As the girl very properly says, Garn! Married indeed! Don't you know that a woman of that class looks a worn out drudge of fifty a year after she's married.

LIZA: Whood marry me?

HIGGINS: [suddenly resorting to the most thrillingly beautiful low tones in his best elocutionary style] By George, Eliza, the streets will be strewn with the bodies of men shooting themselves for your sake before I've done with you.

MRS. PEARCE: Nonsense, sir. You mustn't talk like that to her.

LIZA: [rising and squaring herself determinedly] I'm going away. He's off his chump, he is. I don't want no balmies teaching me.

HIGGINS: [wounded in his tenderest point by her insensibility to his elocution] Oh, indeed! I'm mad, am I? Very well, Mrs. Pearce: you needn't order the new clothes for her. Throw her out.

LIZA: [whimpering] Nah—ow. You got no right to touch me.

MRS. PEARCE: You see now what comes of being saucy. [Indicating the door] This way, please.

LIZA: [almost in tears] I didn't want no clothes. I wouldn't have taken them [she throws away the handkerchief]. I can buy my own clothes.

HIGGINS: [deftly retrieving the handkerchief and intercepting her on her reluctant way to the door] You're an ungrateful wicked girl. This is my return for offering to take you out of the gutter and dress you beautifully and make a lady of you.

MRS. PEARCE: Stop, Mr. Higgins. I won't allow it. It's you that are wicked. Go home to your parents, girl; and tell them to take better care of you.

LIZA: I ain't got no parents. They told me I was big enough to earn my own living and turned me out.

MRS. PEARCE: Where's your mother?

LIZA: I ain't got no mother. Her that turned me out was my sixth stepmother. But I done without them. And I'm a good girl, I am.

HIGGINS: Very well, then, what on earth is all this fuss about? The girl doesn't belong to anybody—is no use to anybody but me. *[He goes to Mrs. Pearce and begins coaxing].* You can adopt her, Mrs. Pearce. I'm sure a daughter would be a great amusement to you. Now don't make any more fuss. Take her downstairs; and—

MRS. PEARCE: But what's to become of her? Is she to be paid anything? Do be sensible, sir.

HIGGINS: Oh, pay her whatever is necessary: put it down in the housekeeping book. *[Impatiently]* What on earth will she want with money? She'll have her food and her clothes. She'll only drink if you give her money.

LIZA: *[turning on him]* Oh you are a brute. It's a lie: nobody ever saw the sign of liquor on me. *[She goes back to her chair and plants herself there defiantly].*

PICKERING: *[in good-humored remonstrance]* Does it occur to you, Higgins, that the girl has some feelings?

HIGGINS: *[looking critically at her]* Oh no, I don't think so. Not any feelings that we need bother about. *[Cheerily]* Have you, Eliza?

LIZA: I got my feelings same as anyone else.

HIGGINS: *[to Pickering, reflectively]* You see the difficulty?

PICKERING: Eh? What difficulty?

HIGGINS: To get her to talk grammar. The mere pronunciation is easy enough.

LIZA: I don't want to talk grammar. I want to talk like a lady.

MRS. PEARCE: Will you please keep to the point, Mr. Higgins. I want to know on what terms the girl is to be here. Is she to have any wages? And what is to become of her when you've finished your teaching? You must look ahead a little.

HIGGINS: *[impatiently]* What's to become of her if I leave her in the gutter? Tell me that, Mrs. Pearce.

MRS. PEARCE: That's her own business, not yours, Mr. Higgins.

HIGGINS: Well, when I've done with her, we can throw her back into the gutter; and then it will be her own business again; so that's all right.

LIZA: Oh, you've no feeling heart in you: you don't care for nothing but yourself *[she rises and takes the floor resolutely].* Here! I've had enough of this. I'm going *[making for the door].* You ought to be ashamed of yourself, you ought.

HIGGINS: *[snatching a chocolate cream from the piano, his eyes suddenly beginning to twinkle with mischief]* Have some chocolates, Eliza.

LIZA: *[halting, tempted]* How do I know what might be in them? I've heard of girls being drugged by the like of you.

[Higgins whips out his penknife; cuts a chocolate in two; puts one half into his mouth and bolts it; and offers her the other half.]

HIGGINS: Pledge of good faith, Eliza. I eat one half you eat the other.
[Liza opens her mouth to retort: he pops the half chocolate into it]. You shall have boxes of them, barrels of them, every day. You shall live on them. Eh?

LIZA: *[who has disposed of the chocolate after being nearly choked by it]* I wouldn't have ate it, only I'm too ladylike to take it out of my mouth.

HIGGINS: Listen, Eliza. I think you said you came in a taxi.

LIZA: Well, what if I did? I've as good a right to take a taxi as anyone else.

HIGGINS: You have, Eliza; and in future you shall have as many taxis as you want. You shall go up and down and round the town in a taxi every day. Think of that, Eliza.

MRS. PEARCE: Mr. Higgins: you're tempting the girl. It's not right. She should think of the future.

HIGGINS: At her age! Nonsense! Time enough to think of the future when you haven't any future to think of. No, Eliza: do as this lady does: think of other people's futures; but never think of your own. Think of chocolates, and taxis, and gold, and diamonds.

LIZA: No: I don't want no gold and no diamonds. I'm a good girl, I am. *[She sits down again, with an attempt at dignity]*.

HIGGINS: You shall remain so, Eliza, under the care of Mrs. Pearce. And you shall marry an officer in the Guards, with a beautiful moustache: the son of a marquis, who will disinherit him for marrying you, but will relent when he sees your beauty and goodness—

PICKERING: Excuse me, Higgins; but I really must interfere. Mrs. Pearce is quite right. If this girl is to put herself in your hands for six months for an experiment in teaching, she must understand thoroughly what she's doing.

HIGGINS: How can she? She's incapable of understanding anything. Besides, do any of us understand what we are doing? If we did, would we ever do it?

PICKERING: Very clever, Higgins; but not sound sense. *[To Eliza]* Miss Doolittle—

LIZA: *[overwhelmed]* Ah—ah—ow—oo!

HIGGINS: There! That's all you get out of Eliza. Ah—ah—ow—oo! No use explaining. As a military man you ought to know that. Give her her orders: that's what she wants. Eliza: you are to live here for the next six months, learning how to speak beautifully, like a lady in a florist's shop. If you're good and do whatever you're told, you shall sleep in a proper bedroom, and have lots to eat, and money to buy chocolates and take rides in taxis. If you're naughty and idle you will sleep in the back kitchen among the black beetles, and be walloped by Mrs. Pearce with a broomstick. At the end of six months you shall go to Buckingham Palace[†] in a carriage, beautifully dressed. If the King finds out you're not a lady, you will be taken by the police to the Tower of London,[†] where your head will be cut off as a warning to other presumptuous flower girls. If you are not found out, you shall have a present of seven-and-sixpence to start life with as a lady in a shop. If you refuse this offer you will be a most ungrateful and wicked girl; and the angels will weep for you. *[To Pickering]* Now are you satisfied, Pickering? *[To Mrs. Pearce]* Can I put it more plainly and fairly, Mrs. Pearce?

MRS. PEARCE: *[patiently]* I think you'd better let me speak to the girl properly in private. I don't know that I can take charge of her or consent to the arrangement at all. Of course I know you don't mean her any harm; but when you get what you call interested in people's accents, you never think or care what may happen to them or you. Come with me, Eliza.

HIGGINS: That's all right. Thank you, Mrs. Pearce. Bundle her off to the bath-room.

LIZA: *[rising reluctantly and suspiciously]* You're a great bully, you are. I won't stay here if I don't like. I won't let nobody wallop me. I never asked to go to Bucknam Palace, I didn't. I was never in trouble with the police, not me. I'm a good girl—

MRS. PEARCE: Don't answer back, girl. You don't understand the gentleman. Come with me. *[She leads the way to the door, and holds it open for Eliza]*.

LIZA: *[as she goes out]* Well, what I say is right. I won't go near the king, not if I'm going to have my head cut off. If I'd known what I was letting myself in for, I wouldn't have come here. I always been a good girl; and I never offered to say a word to him; and I don't owe him nothing; and I don't care; and I won't be put upon; and I have my feelings the same as anyone else—

[Mrs. Pearce shuts the door; and Eliza's plaints are no longer audible. Pickering comes from the hearth to the chair and sits astride it with his arms on the back.]

PICKERING: Excuse the straight question, Higgins. Are you a man of good character where women are concerned?

HIGGINS: *[moodily]* Have you ever met a man of good character where women are concerned?

PICKERING: Yes: very frequently.

HIGGINS: *[dogmatically, lifting himself on his hands to the level of the piano, and sitting on it with a bounce]* Well, I haven't. I find that the moment I let a woman make friends with me, she becomes jealous, exacting, suspicious, and a damned nuisance. I find that the moment I let myself make friends with a woman, I become selfish and tyrannical. Women upset everything. When you let them into your life, you find that the woman is driving at one thing and you're driving at another.

PICKERING: At what, for example?

HIGGINS: *[coming off the piano restlessly]* Oh, Lord knows! I suppose the woman wants to live her own life; and the man wants to live his; and each tries to drag the other on to the wrong track. One wants to go north and the other south; and the result is that both have to go east, though they both hate the east wind. *[He sits down on the bench at the keyboard]*. So here I am, a confirmed old bachelor, and likely to remain so.

PICKERING: *[rising and standing over him gravely]* Come, Higgins! You know what I mean. If I'm to be in this business I shall feel responsible for that girl. I hope it's understood that no advantage is to be taken of her position.

HIGGINS: What! That thing! Sacred, I assure you. *[Rising to explain]* You see, she'll be a pupil; and teaching would be impossible unless pupils were sacred. I've taught scores of American millionairesses how to speak English: the best looking women in the world. I'm seasoned. They might as well be blocks of wood. I might as well be a block of wood. It's—

[Mrs. Pearce opens the door. She has Eliza's hat in her hand. Pickering retires to the easy-chair at the hearth and sits down.]

HIGGINS: *[eagerly]* Well, Mrs. Pearce is it all right?

MRS. PEARCE: *[at the door]* I just wish to trouble you with a word, if I may, Mr. Higgins.

HIGGINS: Yes, certainly. Come in. *[She comes forward].* Don't burn that, Mrs. Pearce. I'll keep it as a curiosity. *[He takes the hat].*

MRS. PEARCE: Handle it carefully, sir, please. I had to promise her not to burn it; but I had better put it in the oven for a while.

HIGGINS: *[putting it down hastily on the piano]* Oh! thank you. Well, what have you to say to me?

PICKERING: Am I in the way?

MRS. PEARCE: Not at all, sir. Mr. Higgins: will you please be very particular what you say before the girl?

HIGGINS: *[sternly]* Of course. I'm always particular about what I say. Why do you say this to me?

MRS. PEARCE: *[unmoved]* No, sir: you're not at all particular when you've mislaid anything or when you get a little impatient. Now it doesn't matter before me: I'm used to it. But you really must not swear before the girl.

HIGGINS: *[indignantly]* I swear! *[Most emphatically]* I never swear. I detest the habit. What the devil do you mean?

MRS. PEARCE: *[stolidly]* That's what I mean, sir. You swear a great deal too much. I don't mind your damning and blasting, and what the devil and where the devil and who the devil—

HIGGINS: Mrs. Pearce: this language from your lips! Really!

MRS. PEARCE: *[not to be put off]*—but there is a certain word I must ask you not to use. The girl has just used it herself because the bath was too hot. It begins with the same letter as bath. She knows no better: she learnt it at her mother's knee. But she must not hear it from your lips.

HIGGINS: *[loftily]* I cannot charge myself with having ever uttered it, Mrs. Pearce. *[She looks at him steadfastly. He adds, hiding an uneasy conscience with a judicial air]* Except perhaps in a moment of extreme and justifiable excitement.

MRS. PEARCE: Only this morning, sir, you applied it to your boots, to the butter, and to the brown bread.

HIGGINS: Oh, that! Mere alliteration, Mrs. Pearce, natural to a poet.

MRS. PEARCE: Well, sir, whatever you choose to call it, I beg you not to let the girl hear you repeat it.

HIGGINS: Oh, very well, very well. Is that all?

MRS. PEARCE: No, sir. We shall have to be very particular with this girl as to personal cleanliness.

HIGGINS: Certainly. Quite right. Most important.

MRS. PEARCE: I mean not to be slovenly about her dress or untidy in leaving things about.

HIGGINS: [going to her solemnly] Just so. I intended to call your attention to that [He passes on to Pickering, who is enjoying the conversation immensely]. It is these little things that matter, Pickering. Take care of the pence and the pounds will take care of themselves is as true of personal habits as of money. [He comes to anchor on the hearthrug, with the air of a man in an unassailable position].

MRS. PEARCE: Yes, sir. Then might I ask you not to come down to breakfast in your dressing-gown, or at any rate not to use it as a napkin to the extent you do, sir. And if you would be so good as not to eat everything off the same plate, and to remember not to put the porridge saucepan out of your hand on the clean tablecloth, it would be a better example to the girl. You know you nearly choked yourself with a fishbone in the jam only last week.

HIGGINS: [routed from the hearthrug and drifting back to the piano] I may do these things sometimes in absence of mind; but surely I don't do them habitually. [Angrily] By the way: my dressing-gown smells most damnably of benzine.

MRS. PEARCE: No doubt it does, Mr. Higgins. But if you will wipe your fingers—

HIGGINS: [yelling] Oh very well, very well: I'll wipe them in my hair in future.

MRS. PEARCE: I hope you're not offended, Mr. Higgins.

HIGGINS: [shocked at finding himself thought capable of an unamiable sentiment] Not at all, not at all. You're quite right, Mrs. Pearce: I shall be particularly careful before the girl. Is that all?

MRS. PEARCE: No, sir. Might she use some of those Japanese dresses you brought from abroad? I really can't put her back into her old things.

HIGGINS: Certainly. Anything you like. Is that all?

MRS. PEARCE: Thank you, sir. That's all. [She goes out].

HIGGINS: You know, Pickering, that woman has the most extraordinary ideas about me. Here I am, a shy, diffident sort of man. I've never been able to feel really grown-up and tremendous, like other chaps. And yet she's firmly persuaded that I'm an arbitrary overbearing bossing kind of person. I can't account for it.

[Mrs. Pearce returns.]

MRS. PEARCE: If you please, sir, the trouble's beginning already. There's a dustman downstairs, Alfred Doolittle, wants to see you. He says you have his daughter here.

PICKERING: [*rising*] Phew! I say! [*He retreats to the hearthrug*].

HIGGINS: [*promptly*] Send the blackguard up.

MRS. PEARCE: Oh, very well, sir. [*She goes out*].

PICKERING: He may not be a blackguard, Higgins.

HIGGINS: Nonsense. Of course he's a blackguard.

PICKERING: Whether he is or not, I'm afraid we shall have some trouble with him.

HIGGINS: [*confidently*] Oh no: I think not. If there's any trouble he shall have it with me, not I with him. And we are sure to get something interesting out of him.

PICKERING: About the girl?

HIGGINS: No. I mean his dialect.

PICKERING: Oh!

MRS. PEARCE: [*at the door*] Doolittle, sir. [*She admits Doolittle and retires*].

[*Alfred Doolittle is an elderly but vigorous dustman, clad in the costume of his profession, including a hat with a back brim covering his neck and shoulders. He has well marked and rather interesting features, and seems equally free from fear and conscience. He has a remarkably expressive voice, the result of a habit of giving vent to his feelings without reserve. His present pose is that of wounded honor and stern resolution.*]

DOOLITTLE: [*at the door, uncertain which of the two gentlemen is his man*] Professor Higgins?

HIGGINS: Here. Good morning. Sit down.

DOOLITTLE: Morning, Governor. [*He sits down magisterially*] I come about a very serious matter, Governor.

HIGGINS: [*to Pickering*] Brought up in Hounslow. Mother Welsh, I should think. [*Doolittle opens his mouth, amazed. Higgins continues*] What do you want, Doolittle?

DOOLITTLE: [*menacingly*] I want my daughter: that's what I want. See?

HIGGINS: Of course you do. You're her father, aren't you? You don't suppose anyone else wants her, do you? I'm glad to see you have some spark of family feeling left. She's upstairs. Take her away at once.

DOOLITTLE: [*rising, fearfully taken aback*] What!

HIGGINS: Take her away. Do you suppose I'm going to keep your daughter for you?

DOOLITTLE: [remonstrating] Now, now, look here, Governor. Is this reasonable? Is it fairity to take advantage of a man like this? The girl belongs to me. You got her. Where do I come in? [He sits down again].

HIGGINS: Your daughter had the audacity to come to my house and ask me to teach her how to speak properly so that she could get a place in a flower-shop. This gentleman and my housekeeper have been here all the time. [Bullying him] How dare you come here and attempt to black-mail me? You sent her here on purpose.

DOOLITTLE: [protesting] No, Governor.

HIGGINS: You must have. How else could you possibly know that she is here?

DOOLITTLE: Don't take a man up like that, Governor.

HIGGINS: The police shall take you up. This is a plant—a plot to extort money by threats. I shall telephone for the police [he goes resolutely to the telephone and opens the directory].

DOOLITTLE: Have I asked you for a brass farthing? I leave it to the gentleman here: have I said a word about money?

HIGGINS: [throwing the book aside and marching down on Doolittle with a poser] What else did you come for?

DOOLITTLE: [sweetly] Well, what would a man come for? Be human, Governor.

HIGGINS: [disarmed] Alfred: did you put her up to it?

DOOLITTLE: So help me, Governor, I never did. I take my Bible oath I ain't seen the girl these two months past.

HIGGINS: Then how did you know she was here?

DOOLITTLE: ["most musical, most melancholy"] I'll tell you, Governor, if you'll only let me get a word in. I'm willing to tell you. I'm wanting to tell you. I'm waiting to tell you.

HIGGINS: Pickering: this chap has a certain natural gift of rhetoric. Observe the rhythm of his native woodnotes wild. "I'm willing to tell you: I'm wanting to tell you: I'm waiting to tell you." Sentimental rhetoric! That's the Welsh strain in him. It also accounts for his mendacity and dishonesty.

PICKERING: Oh, please, Higgins: I'm west country myself. [To Doolittle] How did you know the girl was here if you didn't send her?

DOOLITTLE: It was like this, Governor. The girl took a boy in the taxi to give him a jaunt. Son of her landlady, he is. He hung about on the chance of her giving him another ride home. Well, she sent him back for her luggage when she heard you was willing for her to stop here. I met the boy at the corner of Long Acre and Endell Street.

HIGGINS: Public house. Yes?

DOOLITTLE: The poor man's club, Governor: why shouldn't I?

PICKERING: Do let him tell his story, Higgins.

DOOLITTLE: He told me what was up. And I ask you, what was my feelings and my duty as a father? I says to the boy, "You bring me the luggage," I says—

PICKERING: Why didn't you go for it yourself?

DOOLITTLE: Landlady wouldn't have trusted me with it, Governor. She's that kind of woman: you know. I had to give the boy a penny afore he trusted me with it, the little swine. I brought it to her just to oblige you like, and make myself agreeable. That's all.

HIGGINS: How much luggage?

DOOLITTLE: Musical instrument, Governor. A few pictures, a trifle of jewelry, and a bird-cage. She said she didn't want no clothes. What was I to think from that, Governor? I ask you as a parent what was I to think?

HIGGINS: So you came to rescue her from worse than death, eh?

DOOLITTLE: [appreciatively: relieved at being understood] Just so, Governor. That's right.

PICKERING: But why did you bring her luggage if you intended to take her away?

DOOLITTLE: Have I said a word about taking her away? Have I now?

HIGGINS: [determinedly] You're going to take her away, double quick. [He crosses to the hearth and rings the bell].

DOOLITTLE: [rising] No, Governor. Don't say that. I'm not the man to stand in my girl's light. Here's a career opening for her, as you might say; and—

[Mrs. Pearce opens the door and awaits orders.]

HIGGINS: Mrs. Pearce: this is Eliza's father. He has come to take her away. Give her to him. [He goes back to the piano, with an air of washing his hands of the whole affair].

DOOLITTLE: No. This is a misunderstanding. Listen here—

MRS. PEARCE: He can't take her away, Mr. Higgins: how can he? You told me to burn her clothes.

DOOLITTLE: That's right. I can't carry the girl through the streets like a blooming monkey, can I? I put it to you.

HIGGINS: You have put it to me that you want your daughter. Take your daughter. If she has no clothes go out and buy her some.

DOOLITTLE: [desperate] Where's the clothes she come in? Did I burn them or did your missus here?

MRS. PEARCE: I am the housekeeper, if you please. I have sent for some clothes for your girl. When they come you can take her away. You can wait in the kitchen. This way, please.

[Doolittle, much troubled, accompanies her to the door; then hesitates; finally turns confidentially to Higgins.]

DOOLITTLE: Listen here, Governor. You and me is men of the world, ain't we?

HIGGINS: Oh! Men of the world, are we? You'd better go, Mrs. Pearce.

MRS. PEARCE: I think so, indeed, sir. [She goes, with dignity].

PICKERING: The floor is yours, Mr. Doolittle.

DOOLITTLE: [to Pickering] I thank you, Governor. [To Higgins, who takes refuge on the piano bench, a little overwhelmed by the proximity of his visitor; for Doolittle has a professional flavor of dust about him]. Well, the truth is, I've taken a sort of fancy to you, Governor; and if you want the girl, I'm not so set on having her back home again but what I might be open to an arrangement. Regarded in the light of a young woman, she's a fine handsome girl. As a daughter she's not worth her keep; and so I tell you straight. All I ask is my rights as a father; and you're the last man alive to expect me to let her go for nothing; for I can see you're one of the straight sort, Governor. Well, what's a five pound note to you? And what's Eliza to me? [He returns to his chair and sits down judicially].

PICKERING: I think you ought to know, Doolittle, that Mr. Higgins's intentions are entirely honorable.

DOOLITTLE: Course they are, Governor. If I thought they wasn't, I'd ask fifty.

HIGGINS: [revolted] Do you mean to say, you callous rascal, that you would sell your daughter for £50?

DOOLITTLE: Not in a general way I wouldn't; but to oblige a gentleman like you I'd do a good deal, I do assure you.

PICKERING: Have you no morals, man?

DOOLITTLE: [unabashed] Can't afford them, Governor. Neither could you if you was as poor as me. Not that I mean any harm, you know. But if Liza is going to have a bit out of this, why not me too?

HIGGINS: [troubled] I don't know what to do, Pickering. There can be no question that as a matter of morals it's a positive crime to give this chap a farthing. And yet I feel a sort of rough justice in his claim.

DOOLITTLE: That's it, Governor. That's all I say. A father's heart, as it were.

PICKERING: Well, I know the feeling; but really it seems hardly right—

DOOLITTLE: Don't say that, Governor. Don't look at it that way. What am I, Governors both? I ask you, what am I? I'm one of the undeserving poor: that's what I am. Think of what that means to a man. It means that he's up agen middle class morality all the time. If there's anything going, and I put in for a bit of it, it's always the same story: "You're undeserving; so you can't have it." But my needs is as great as the most deserving widow's that ever got money out of six different charities in one week for the death of the same husband. I don't need less than a deserving man: I need more. I don't eat less hearty than him; and I drink a lot more. I want a bit of amusement, cause I'm a thinking man. I want cheerfulness and a song and a band when I feel low. Well, they charge me just the same for everything as they charge the deserving. What is middle class morality? Just an excuse for never giving me anything. Therefore, I ask you, as two gentlemen, not to play that game on me. I'm playing straight with you. I ain't pretending to be deserving. I'm undeserving; and I mean to go on being undeserving. I like it; and that's the truth. Will you take advantage of a man's nature to do him out of the price of his own daughter what he's brought up and fed and clothed by the sweat of his brow until she's growed big enough to be interesting to you two gentlemen? Is five pounds unreasonable? I put it to you; and I leave it to you.

HIGGINS: [rising, and going over to Pickering] Pickering: if we were to take this man in hand for three months, he could choose between a seat in the Cabinet and a popular pulpit in Wales.†

PICKERING: What do you say to that, Doolittle?

DOOLITTLE: Not me, Governor, thank you kindly. I've heard all the preachers and all the prime ministers—for I'm a thinking man and game for politics or religion or social reform same as all the other amusements—and I tell you it's a dog's life anyway you look at it.

Undeserving poverty is my line. Taking one station in society with another, it's—it's—well, it's the only one that has any ginger in it, to my taste.

HIGGINS: I suppose we must give him a fiver.

PICKERING: He'll make a bad use of it, I'm afraid.

DOOLITTLE: Not me, Governor, so help me I won't. Don't you be afraid that I'll save it and spare it and live idle on it. There won't be a penny of it left by Monday: I'll have to go to work same as if I'd never had it. It won't pauperize me, you bet. Just one good spree for myself and the missus, giving pleasure to ourselves and employment to others, and satisfaction to you to think it's not been throwed away. You couldn't spend it better.

HIGGINS: [taking out his pocket book and coming between Doolittle and the piano] This is irresistible. Let's give him ten. [He offers two notes to the dustman].

DOOLITTLE: No, Governor. She wouldn't have the heart to spend ten; and perhaps I shouldn't neither. Ten pounds is a lot of money: it makes a man feel prudent like; and then goodbye to happiness. You give me what I ask you, Governor: not a penny more, and not a penny less.

PICKERING: Why don't you marry that missus of yours? I rather draw the line at encouraging that sort of immorality.

DOOLITTLE: Tell her so, Governor: tell her so. I'm willing. It's me that suffers by it. I've no hold on her. I got to be agreeable to her. I got to give her presents. I got to buy her clothes something sinful. I'm a slave to that woman, Governor, just because I'm not her lawful husband. And she knows it too. Catch her marrying me! Take my advice, Governor: marry Eliza while she's young and don't know no better. If you don't you'll be sorry for it after. If you do, she'll be sorry for it after; but better you than her, because you're a man, and she's only a woman and don't know how to be happy anyhow.

HIGGINS: Pickering: if we listen to this man another minute, we shall have no convictions left. [To Doolittle] Five pounds I think you said.

DOOLITTLE: Thank you kindly, Governor.

HIGGINS: You're sure you won't take ten?

DOOLITTLE: Not now. Another time, Governor.

HIGGINS: [handing him a five-pound note] Here you are.

DOOLITTLE: Thank you, Governor. Good morning. [He hurries to the door, anxious to get away with his booty. When he opens it he is confronted with a dainty and exquisitely clean young Japanese lady in a simple blue cotton *kimono printed cunningly with small white jasmine blossoms. Mrs. Pearce is with her. He gets out of her way deferentially and apologizes].* Beg pardon, miss.

THE JAPANESE LADY: Garn! Don't you know your own daughter?

DOOLITTLE: }	*exclaiming*	Bly me! it's Eliza!
HIGGINS: }	*simul-*	What's that! This!
PICKERING: }	*taneously*	By Jove!

LIZA: Don't I look silly?

HIGGINS: Silly?

MRS. PEARCE: *[at the door]* Now, Mr. Higgins, please don't say anything to make the girl conceited about herself.

HIGGINS: *[conscientiously]* Oh! Quite right, Mrs. Pearce. *[To Eliza]* Yes: damned silly.

MRS. PEARCE: Please, sir.

HIGGINS: *[correcting himself]* I mean extremely silly.

LIZA: I should look all right with my hat on. *[She takes up her hat; puts it on; and walks across the room to the fireplace with a fashionable air].*

HIGGINS: A new fashion, by George! And it ought to look horrible!

DOOLITTLE: *[with fatherly pride]* Well, I never thought she'd clean up as good looking as that, Governor. She's a credit to me, ain't she?

LIZA: I tell you, it's easy to clean up here. Hot and cold water on tap, just as much as you like, there is. Woolly towels, there is; and a towel horse so hot, it burns your fingers. Soft brushes to scrub yourself, and a wooden bowl of soap smelling like primroses. Now I know why ladies is so clean. Washing's a treat for them. Wish they saw what it is for the like of me!

HIGGINS: I'm glad the bath-room met with your approval.

LIZA: It didn't: not all of it; and I don't care who hears me say it. Mrs. Pearce knows.

HIGGINS: What was wrong, Mrs. Pearce?

MRS. PEARCE: *[blandly]* Oh, nothing, sir. It doesn't matter.

LIZA: I had a good mind to break it. I didn't know which way to look. But I hung a towel over it, I did.

HIGGINS: Over what?

MRS. PEARCE: Over the looking-glass, sir.

HIGGINS: Doolittle: you have brought your daughter up too strictly.

DOOLITTLE: Me! I never brought her up at all, except to give her a lick of a strap now and again. Don't put it on me, Governor. She ain't accustomed to it, you see: that's all. But she'll soon pick up your free-and-easy ways.

LIZA: I'm a good girl, I am; and I won't pick up no free and easy ways.

HIGGINS: Eliza: if you say again that you're a good girl, your father shall take you home.

LIZA: Not him. You don't know my father. All he come here for was to touch you for some money to get drunk on.

DOOLITTLE: Well, what else would I want money for? To put into the plate in church, I suppose. *[She puts out her tongue at him. He is so incensed by this that Pickering presently finds it necessary to step between them]*. Don't you give me none of your lip; and don't let me hear you giving this gentleman any of it neither, or you'll hear from me about it. See?

HIGGINS: Have you any further advice to give her before you go, Doolittle? Your blessing, for instance.

DOOLITTLE: No, Governor: I ain't such a mug as to put up my children to all I know myself. Hard enough to hold them in without that. If you want Eliza's mind improved, Governor, you do it yourself with a strap. So long, gentlemen. *[He turns to go]*.

HIGGINS: *[impressively]* Stop. You'll come regularly to see your daughter. It's your duty, you know. My brother is a clergyman; and he could help you in your talks with her.

DOOLITTLE: *[evasively]* Certainly. I'll come, Governor. Not just this week, because I have a job at a distance. But later on you may depend on me. Afternoon, gentlemen. Afternoon, ma'am. *[He takes off his hat to Mrs. Pearce, who disdains the salutation and goes out. He winks at Higgins, thinking him probably a fellow sufferer from Mrs. Pearce's difficult disposition, and follows her]*.

LIZA: Don't you believe the old liar. He'd as soon you set a bull-dog on him as a clergyman. You won't see him again in a hurry.

HIGGINS: I don't want to, Eliza. Do you?

LIZA: Not me. I don't want never to see him again, I don't. He's a disgrace to me, he is, collecting dust, instead of working at his trade.

PICKERING: What is his trade, Eliza?

LIZA: Talking money out of other people's pockets into his own. His proper trade's a navvy; and he works at it sometimes too—for exercise—and earns good money at it. Ain't you going to call me Miss Doolittle any more?

PICKERING: I beg your pardon, Miss Doolittle. It was a slip of the tongue.

LIZA: Oh, I don't mind; only it sounded so genteel. I should just like to take a taxi to the corner of Tottenham Court Road and get out there and tell it to wait for me, just to put the girls in their place a bit. I wouldn't speak to them, you know.

PICKERING: Better wait til we get you something really fashionable.

HIGGINS: Besides, you shouldn't cut your old friends now that you have risen in the world. That's what we call snobbery.

LIZA: You don't call the like of them my friends now, I should hope. They've took it out of me often enough with their ridicule when they had the chance; and now I mean to get a bit of my own back. But if I'm to have fashionable clothes, I'll wait. I should like to have some. Mrs. Pearce says you're going to give me some to wear in bed at night different to what I wear in the daytime; but it do seem a waste of money when you could get something to show. Besides, I never could fancy changing into cold things on a winter night.

MRS. PEARCE: [coming back] Now, Eliza. The new things have come for you to try on.

LIZA: Ah—ow—oo—ooh! [She rushes out].

MRS. PEARCE: [following her] Oh, don't rush about like that, girl [She shuts the door behind her].

HIGGINS: Pickering: we have taken on a stiff job.

PICKERING: [with conviction] Higgins: we have.

Act III

[It is Mrs. Higgins's at-home day. Nobody has yet arrived. Her drawing-room, in a flat on Chelsea embankment, has three windows looking on the river; and the ceiling is not so lofty as it would be in an older house of the same pretension. The windows are open, giving access to a balcony with flowers in pots. If you stand with your face to the windows, you have the fireplace on your left and the door in the right-hand wall close to the corner nearest the windows.

Mrs. Higgins was brought up on Morris and Burne Jones; and her room, which is very unlike her son's room in Wimpole Street, is not crowded with furniture and little tables and nicknacks. In the middle of the room there is a big ottoman; and this, with the carpet, the Morris wall-papers, and the Morris chintz window curtains† and brocade covers of the ottoman and its cushions, supply all the ornament, and are much too handsome to be hidden by odds and ends of useless things. A few good oil-paintings from the exhibitions in the Grosvenor Gallery† thirty years ago (the Burne Jones,† not the Whistler† side of them) are on the walls. The only landscape is a Cecil Lawson† on the scale of a Rubens.† There is a portrait of Mrs. Higgins as she was when she defied fashion in her youth in one of the beautiful Rossettian costumes which, when caricatured by people who did not understand, led to the absurdities of popular estheticism in the eighteen-seventies.

In the corner diagonally opposite the door Mrs. Higgins, now over sixty and long past taking the trouble to dress out of the fashion, sits writing at an elegantly simple writing-table with a bell button within reach of her hand. There is a Chippendale chair† further back in the room between her and the window

49

nearest her side. At the other side of the room, further forward, is an Elizabethan
chair roughly carved in the taste of Inigo Jones.[†] On the same side a piano in a
decorated case. The corner between the fireplace and the window is occupied by
a divan cushioned in Morris chintz.

> *It is between four and five in the afternoon.*
> *The door is opened violently; and Higgins enters with his hat on.]*

MRS. HIGGINS: *[dismayed]* Henry! *[scolding him]* What are you doing here
to-day? It is my at-home day: you promised not to come. *[As he bends
to kiss her, she takes his hat off, and presents it to him].*

HIGGINS: Oh bother! *[He throws the hat down on the table].*

MRS. HIGGINS: Go home at once.

HIGGINS: *[kissing her]* I know, mother. I came on purpose.

MRS. HIGGINS: But you mustn't. I'm serious, Henry. You offend all my
friends: they stop coming whenever they meet you.

HIGGINS: Nonsense! I know I have no small talk; but people don't mind.
[He sits on the settee].

MRS. HIGGINS: Oh! don't they? Small talk indeed! What about your large
talk? Really, dear, you mustn't stay.

HIGGINS: I must. I've a job for you. A phonetic job.

MRS. HIGGINS: No use, dear. I'm sorry; but I can't get round your vowels;
and though I like to get pretty postcards in your patent shorthand, I
always have to read the copies in ordinary writing you so thoughtfully
send me.

HIGGINS: Well, this isn't a phonetic job.

MRS. HIGGINS: You said it was.

HIGGINS: Not your part of it. I've picked up a girl.

MRS. HIGGINS: Does that mean that some girl has picked you up?

HIGGINS: Not at all. I don't mean a love affair.

MRS. HIGGINS: What a pity!

HIGGINS: Why?

MRS. HIGGINS: Well, you never fall in love with anyone under forty-five.
When will you discover that there are some rather nice-looking young
women about?

HIGGINS: Oh, I can't be bothered with young women. My idea of a loveable
woman is something as like you as possible. I shall never get into the
way of seriously liking young women: some habits lie too deep to be
changed. *[Rising abruptly and walking about, jingling his money and his keys
in his trouser pockets]* Besides, they're all idiots.

MRS. HIGGINS: Do you know what you would do if you really loved me, Henry?

HIGGINS: Oh bother! What? Marry, I suppose?

MRS. HIGGINS: No. Stop fidgeting and take your hands out of your pockets. *[With a gesture of despair, he obeys and sits down again]*. That's a good boy. Now tell me about the girl.

HIGGINS: She's coming to see you.

MRS. HIGGINS: I don't remember asking her.

HIGGINS: You didn't. I asked her. If you'd known her you wouldn't have asked her.

MRS. HIGGINS: Indeed! Why?

HIGGINS: Well, it's like this. She's a common flower girl. I picked her off the kerbstone.

MRS. HIGGINS: And invited her to my at-home!

HIGGINS: *[rising and coming to her to coax her]* Oh, that'll be all right. I've taught her to speak properly; and she has strict orders as to her behavior. She's to keep to two subjects: the weather and everybody's health —Fine day and How do you do, you know —and not to let herself go on things in general. That will be safe.

MRS. HIGGINS: Safe! To talk about our health! about our insides! perhaps about our outsides! How could you be so silly, Henry?

HIGGINS: *[impatiently]* Well, she must talk about something. *[He controls himself and sits down again]*. Oh, she'll be all right: don't you fuss. Pickering is in it with me. I've a sort of bet on that I'll pass her off as a duchess in six months. I started on her some months ago; and she's getting on like a house on fire. I shall win my bet. She has a quick ear; and she's been easier to teach than my middle-class pupils because she's had to learn a complete new language. She talks English almost as you talk French.

MRS. HIGGINS: That's satisfactory, at all events.

HIGGINS: Well, it is and it isn't.

MRS. HIGGINS: What does that mean?

HIGGINS: You see, I've got her pronunciation all right; but you have to consider not only how a girl pronounces, but what she pronounces; and that's where—

[They are interrupted by the parlor-maid, announcing guests.]

THE PARLOR-MAID: Mrs. and Miss Eynsford Hill. *[She withdraws]*.

HIGGINS: Oh Lord! *[He rises; snatches his hat from the table; and makes for the door; but before he reaches it his mother introduces him].*

[Mrs. and Miss Eynsford Hill are the mother and daughter who sheltered from the rain in Covent Garden. The mother is well bred, quiet, and has the habitual anxiety of straitened means. The daughter has acquired a gay air of being very much at home in society: the bravado of genteel poverty.]

MRS. EYNSFORD HILL: *[to Mrs. Higgins]* How do you do? *[They shake hands].*
MISS EYNSFORD HILL: How d'you do? *[She shakes].*
MRS. HIGGINS: *[introducing]* My son Henry.
MRS. EYNSFORD HILL: Your celebrated son! I have so longed to meet you, Professor Higgins.
HIGGINS: *[glumly, making no movement in her direction]* Delighted. *[He backs against the piano and bows brusquely].*
MISS EYNSFORD HILL: *[going to him with confident familiarity]* How do you do?
HIGGINS: *[staring at her]* I've seen you before somewhere. I haven't the ghost of a notion where; but I've heard your voice. *[Drearily]* It doesn't matter. You'd better sit down.
MRS. HIGGINS: I'm sorry to say that my celebrated son has no manners. You mustn't mind him.
MISS EYNSFORD HILL: *[gaily]* I don't. *[She sits in the Elizabethan chair].*
MRS. EYNSFORD HILL: *[a little bewildered]* Not at all. *[She sits on the ottoman between her daughter and Mrs. Higgins, who has turned her chair away from the writing-table].*
HIGGINS: Oh, have I been rude? I didn't mean to be.

[He goes to the central window, through which, with his back to the company, he contemplates the river and the flowers in Battersea Park on the opposite bank as if they were a frozen desert.
The parlor-maid returns, ushering in Pickering.]

THE PARLOR-MAID: Colonel Pickering *[She withdraws].*
PICKERING: How do you do, Mrs. Higgins?
MRS. HIGGINS: So glad you've come. Do you know Mrs. Eynsford Hill— Miss Eynsford Hill? *[Exchange of bows. The Colonel brings the Chippendale chair a little forward between Mrs. Hill and Mrs. Higgins, and sits down].*

PICKERING: Has Henry told you what we've come for?

HIGGINS: *[over his shoulder]* We were interrupted: damn it!

MRS. HIGGINS: Oh Henry, Henry, really!

MRS. EYNSFORD HILL: *[half rising]* Are we in the way?

MRS. HIGGINS:*[rising and making her sit down again]* No, no. You couldn't have come more fortunately: we want you to meet a friend of ours.

HIGGINS:*[turning hopefully]* Yes, by George! We want two or three people. You'll do as well as anybody else.

[The parlor-maid returns, ushering Freddy.]

THE PARLOR-MAID: Mr. Eynsford Hill.

HIGGINS: *[almost audibly, past endurance]* God of Heaven! another of them.

FREDDY: *[shaking hands with Mrs. Higgins]* Ahdedo?

MRS. HIGGINS: Very good of you to come. *[Introducing]* Colonel Pickering.

FREDDY: *[bowing]* Ahdedo?

MRS. HIGGINS: I don't think you know my son, Professor Higgins.

FREDDY: *[going to Higgins]* Ahdedo?

HIGGINS: *[looking at him much as if he were a pickpocket]* I'll take my oath I've met you before somewhere. Where was it?

FREDDY: I don't think so.

HIGGINS: *[resignedly]* It don't matter, anyhow. Sit down.

[He shakes Freddy's hand, and almost slings him on the ottoman with his face to the windows; then comes round to the other side of it.]

HIGGINS: Well, here we are, anyhow! *[He sits down on the ottoman next Mrs. Eynsford Hill, on her left]*. And now, what the devil are we going to talk about until Eliza comes?

MRS. HIGGINS: Henry: you are the life and soul of the Royal Society's soirees;[†] but really you're rather trying on more commonplace occasions.

HIGGINS: Am I? Very sorry. *[Beaming suddenly]* I suppose I am, you know. *[Uproariously]* Ha, ha!

MISS EYNSFORD HILL: *[who considers Higgins quite eligible matrimonially]* I sympathize. I haven't any small talk. If people would only be frank and say what they really think!

HIGGINS: *[relapsing into gloom]* Lord forbid!

MRS. EYNSFORD HILL: *[taking up her daughter's cue]* But why?

HIGGINS: What they think they ought to think is bad enough, Lord knows; but what they really think would break up the whole show. Do you suppose it would be really agreeable if I were to come out now with what I really think?

MISS EYNSFORD HILL: [gaily] Is it so very cynical?

HIGGINS: Cynical! Who the dickens said it was cynical? I mean it wouldn't be decent.

MRS. EYNSFORD HILL: [seriously] Oh! I'm sure you don't mean that, Mr. Higgins.

HIGGINS: You see, we're all savages, more or less. We're supposed to be civilized and cultured—to know all about poetry and philosophy and art and science, and so on; but how many of us know even the meanings of these names? [To Miss Hill] What do you know of poetry? [To Mrs. Hill] What do you know of science? [Indicating Freddy] What does he know of art or science or anything else? What the devil do you imagine I know of philosophy?

MRS. HIGGINS: [warningly] Or of manners, Henry?

THE PARLOR-MAID: [opening the door] Miss Doolittle. [She withdraws].

HIGGINS: [rising hastily and running to Mrs. Higgins] Here she is, mother. [He stands on tiptoe and makes signs over his mother's head to Eliza to indicate to her which lady is her hostess].

[Eliza, who is exquisitely dressed, produces an impression of such remarkable distinction and beauty as she enters that they all rise, quite fluttered. Guided by Higgins's signals, she comes to Mrs. Higgins with studied grace.]

LIZA: [speaking with pedantic correctness of pronunciation and great beauty of tone] How do you do, Mrs. Higgins? [She gasps slightly in making sure of the H in Higgins, but is quite successful]. Mr. Higgins told me I might come.

MRS. HIGGINS: [cordially] Quite right: I'm very glad indeed to see you.

PICKERING: How do you do, Miss Doolittle?

LIZA: [shaking hands with him] Colonel Pickering, is it not?

MRS. EYNSFORD HILL: I feel sure we have met before, Miss Doolittle. I remember your eyes.

LIZA: How do you do? [She sits down on the ottoman gracefully in the place just left vacant by Higgins].

MRS. EYNSFORD HILL: [introducing] My daughter Clara.

LIZA: How do you do?

CLARA: *[impulsively]* How do you do? *[She sits down on the ottoman beside Eliza, devouring her with her eyes].*

FREDDY: *[coming to their side of the ottoman]* I've certainly had the pleasure.

MRS. EYNSFORD HILL: *[introducing]* My son Freddy.

LIZA: How do you do?

[Freddy bows and sits down in the Elizabethan chair, infatuated.]

HIGGINS: *[suddenly]* By George, yes: it all comes back to me! *[They stare at him].* Covent Garden! *[Lamentably]* What a damned thing!

MRS. HIGGINS: Henry, please! *[He is about to sit on the edge of the table].* Don't sit on my writing-table: you'll break it.

HIGGINS: *[sulkily]* Sorry.

[He goes to the divan, stumbling into the fender and over the fire-irons on his way; extricating himself with muttered imprecations; and finishing his disastrous journey by throwing himself so impatiently on the divan that he almost breaks it. Mrs. Higgins looks at him, but controls herself and says nothing.

A long and painful pause ensues.]

MRS. HIGGINS: *[at last, conversationally]* Will it rain, do you think?

LIZA: The shallow depression in the west of these islands is likely to move slowly in an easterly direction. There are no indications of any great change in the barometrical situation.

FREDDY: Ha! ha! how awfully funny!

LIZA: What is wrong with that, young man? I bet I got it right.

FREDDY: Killing!

MRS. EYNSFORD HILL: I'm sure I hope it won't turn cold. There's so much influenza about. It runs right through our whole family regularly every spring.

LIZA: *[darkly]* My aunt died of influenza: so they said.

MRS. EYNSFORD HILL: *[clicks her tongue sympathetically]*!!!

LIZA: *[in the same tragic tone]* But it's my belief they done the old woman in.

MRS. HIGGINS: *[puzzled]* Done her in?

LIZA: Y-e-e-e-es, Lord love you! Why should she die of influenza? She come through diphtheria right enough the year before. I saw her with my own eyes. Fairly blue with it, she was. They all thought she was dead; but my father he kept ladling gin down her throat til she came to so sudden that she bit the bowl off the spoon.

MRS. EYNSFORD HILL: *[startled]* Dear me!

LIZA: *[piling up the indictment]* What call would a woman with that strength in her have to die of influenza? What become of her new straw hat that should have come to me? Somebody pinched it; and what I say is, them as pinched it done her in.

MRS. EYNSFORD HILL: What does doing her in mean?

HIGGINS: *[hastily]* Oh, that's the new small talk. To do a person in means to kill them.

MRS. EYNSFORD HILL: *[to Eliza, horrified]* You surely don't believe that your aunt was killed?

LIZA: Do I not! Them she lived with would have killed her for a hat-pin, let alone a hat.

MRS. EYNSFORD HILL: But it can't have been right for your father to pour spirits down her throat like that. It might have killed her.

LIZA: Not her. Gin was mother's milk to her. Besides, he'd poured so much down his own throat that he knew the good of it.

MRS. EYNSFORD HILL: Do you mean that he drank?

LIZA: Drank! My word! Something chronic.

MRS. EYNSFORD HILL: How dreadful for you!

LIZA: Not a bit. It never did him no harm what I could see. But then he did not keep it up regular. *[Cheerfully]* On the burst, as you might say, from time to time. And always more agreeable when he had a drop in. When he was out of work, my mother used to give him fourpence and tell him to go out and not come back until he'd drunk himself cheerful and loving-like. There's lots of women has to make their husbands drunk to make them fit to live with. *[Now quite at her ease]* You see, it's like this. If a man has a bit of a conscience, it always takes him when he's sober; and then it makes him low-spirited. A drop of booze just takes that off and makes him happy. *[To Freddy, who is in convulsions of suppressed laughter]* Here! what are you sniggering at?

FREDDY: The new small talk. You do it so awfully well.

LIZA: If I was doing it proper, what was you laughing at? *[To Higgins]* Have I said anything I oughtn't?

MRS. HIGGINS: *[interposing]* Not at all, Miss Doolittle.

LIZA: Well, that's a mercy, anyhow. *[Expansively]* What I always say is—

HIGGINS: *[rising and looking at his watch]* Ahem!

LIZA: *[looking round at him; taking the hint; and rising]* Well: I must go. *[They all rise. Freddy goes to the door]*. So pleased to have met you. Good-bye. *[She shakes hands with Mrs. Higgins]*.

MRS. HIGGINS: Good-bye.

LIZA: Good-bye, Colonel Pickering.

PICKERING: Good-bye, Miss Doolittle. *[They shake hands]*.

LIZA: *[nodding to the others]* Good-bye, all.

FREDDY: *[opening the door for her]* Are you walking across the Park, Miss Doolittle? If so—

LIZA: Walk! Not bloody likely. *[Sensation]*. I am going in a taxi. *[She goes out]*.

[Pickering gasps and sits down. Freddy goes out on the balcony to catch another glimpse of Eliza.]

MRS. EYNSFORD HILL: *[suffering from shock]* Well, I really can't get used to the new ways.

CLARA: *[throwing herself discontentedly into the Elizabethan chair]*. Oh, it's all right, mamma, quite right. People will think we never go anywhere or see anybody if you are so old-fashioned.

MRS. EYNSFORD HILL: I daresay I am very old-fashioned; but I do hope you won't begin using that expression, Clara. I have got accustomed to hear you talking about men as rotters, and calling everything filthy and beastly; though I do think it horrible and unladylike. But this last is really too much. Don't you think so, Colonel Pickering?

PICKERING: Don't ask me. I've been away in India for several years; and manners have changed so much that I sometimes don't know whether I'm at a respectable dinner-table or in a ship's forecastle.†

CLARA: It's all a matter of habit. There's no right or wrong in it. Nobody means anything by it. And it's so quaint, and gives such a smart emphasis to things that are not in themselves very witty. I find the new small talk delightful and quite innocent.

MRS. EYNSFORD HILL: *[rising]* Well, after that, I think it's time for us to go.

[Pickering and Higgins rise.]

CLARA: *[rising]* Oh yes: we have three at-homes to go to still. Good-bye, Mrs. Higgins. Good-bye, Colonel Pickering. Good-bye, Professor Higgins.

HIGGINS: *[coming grimly at her from the divan, and accompanying her to the door]* Good-bye. Be sure you try on that small talk at the three at-homes. Don't be nervous about it. Pitch it in strong.

CLARA: *[all smiles]* I will. Good-bye. Such nonsense, all this early Victorian prudery!

HIGGINS: *[tempting her]* Such damned nonsense!

CLARA: Such bloody nonsense!

MRS. EYNSFORD HILL: *[convulsively]* Clara!

CLARA: Ha! ha! *[She goes out radiant, conscious of being thoroughly up to date, and is heard descending the stairs in a stream of silvery laughter]*.

FREDDY: *[to the heavens at large]* Well, I ask you *[He gives it up, and comes to Mrs. Higgins]*. Good-bye.

MRS. HIGGINS: *[shaking hands]* Good-bye. Would you like to meet Miss Doolittle again?

FREDDY: *[eagerly]* Yes, I should, most awfully.

MRS. HIGGINS: Well, you know my days.

FREDDY: Yes. Thanks awfully. Good-bye. *[He goes out]*.

MRS. EYNSFORD HILL: Good-bye, Mr. Higgins.

HIGGINS: Good-bye. Good-bye.

MRS. EYNSFORD HILL: *[to Pickering]* It's no use. I shall never be able to bring myself to use that word.

PICKERING: Don't. It's not compulsory, you know. You'll get on quite well without it.

MRS. EYNSFORD HILL: Only, Clara is so down on me if I am not positively reeking with the latest slang. Good-bye.

PICKERING: Good-bye *[They shake hands]*.

MRS. EYNSFORD HILL: *[to Mrs. Higgins]* You mustn't mind Clara. *[Pickering, catching from her lowered tone that this is not meant for him to hear, discreetly joins Higgins at the window]*. We're so poor! and she gets so few parties, poor child! She doesn't quite know. *[Mrs. Higgins, seeing that her eyes are moist, takes her hand sympathetically and goes with her to the door]*. But the boy is nice. Don't you think so?

MRS. HIGGINS: Oh, quite nice. I shall always be delighted to see him.

MRS. EYNSFORD HILL: Thank you, dear. Good-bye. *[She goes out]*.

HIGGINS: *[eagerly]* Well? Is Eliza presentable? *[he swoops on his mother and drags her to the ottoman, where she sits down in Eliza's place with her son on her left]*

[Pickering returns to his chair on her right.]

MRS. HIGGINS: You silly boy, of course she's not presentable. She's a triumph of your art and of her dressmaker's; but if you suppose for a moment that she doesn't give herself away in every sentence she utters, you must be perfectly cracked about her.

PICKERING: But don't you think something might be done? I mean something to eliminate the sanguinary element from her conversation.

MRS. HIGGINS: Not as long as she is in Henry's hands.

HIGGINS: *[aggrieved]* Do you mean that my language is improper?

MRS. HIGGINS: No, dearest: it would be quite proper—say on a canal barge; but it would not be proper for her at a garden party.

HIGGINS: *[deeply injured]* Well I must say—

PICKERING: *[interrupting him]* Come, Higgins: you must learn to know yourself. I haven't heard such language as yours since we used to review the volunteers in Hyde Park[†] twenty years ago.

HIGGINS: *[sulkily]* Oh, well, if you say so, I suppose I don't always talk like a bishop.

MRS. HIGGINS: *[quieting Henry with a touch]* Colonel Pickering: will you tell me what is the exact state of things in Wimpole Street?

PICKERING: *[cheerfully: as if this completely changed the subject]* Well, I have come to live there with Henry. We work together at my Indian Dialects; and we think it more convenient—

MRS. HIGGINS: Quite so. I know all about that: it's an excellent arrangement. But where does this girl live?

HIGGINS: With us, of course. Where would she live?

MRS. HIGGINS: But on what terms? Is she a servant? If not, what is she?

PICKERING: *[slowly]* I think I know what you mean, Mrs. Higgins.

HIGGINS: Well, dash me if I do! I've had to work at the girl every day for months to get her to her present pitch. Besides, she's useful. She knows where my things are, and remembers my appointments and so forth.

MRS. HIGGINS: How does your housekeeper get on with her?

HIGGINS: Mrs. Pearce? Oh, she's jolly glad to get so much taken off her hands; for before Eliza came, she had to have to find things and remind me of my appointments. But she's got some silly bee in her bonnet about Eliza. She keeps saying "You don't think, sir": doesn't she, Pick?

PICKERING: Yes: that's the formula. "You don't think, sir." That's the end of every conversation about Eliza.

HIGGINS: As if I ever stop thinking about the girl and her confounded vowels and consonants. I'm worn out, thinking about her, and watching her lips and her teeth and her tongue, not to mention her soul, which is the quaintest of the lot.

MRS. HIGGINS: You certainly are a pretty pair of babies, playing with your live doll.

HIGGINS: Playing! The hardest job I ever tackled: make no mistake about that, mother. But you have no idea how frightfully interesting it is to take a human being and change her into a quite different human being by creating a new speech for her. It's filling up the deepest gulf that separates class from class and soul from soul.

PICKERING: [drawing his chair closer to Mrs. Higgins and bending over to her eagerly] Yes: it's enormously interesting. I assure you, Mrs. Higgins, we take Eliza very seriously. Every week—every day almost—there is some new change. [Closer again] We keep records of every stage—dozens of gramophone disks and photographs—

HIGGINS: [assailing her at the other ear] Yes, by George: it's the most absorbing experiment I ever tackled. She regularly fills our lives up; doesn't she, Pick?

PICKERING: We're always talking Eliza.

HIGGINS: Teaching Eliza.

PICKERING: Dressing Eliza.

MRS. HIGGINS: What!

HIGGINS: Inventing new Elizas.

HIGGINS:	[speaking together]	You know, she has the most extraordinary quickness of ear:
PICKERING:		I assure you, my dear Mrs. Higgins, that girl
HIGGINS:		just like a parrot. I've tried her with every
PICKERING:		is a genius. She can play the piano quite beautifully
HIGGINS:		possible sort of sound that a human being can make—
PICKERING:		We have taken her to classical concerts and to music
HIGGINS:		Continental dialects, African dialects, Hottentot
PICKERING:		halls; and it's all the same to her: she plays everything

HIGGINS:		clicks, things it took me years to get hold of; and
PICKERING:		she hears right off when she comes home, whether it's
HIGGINS:	*[speaking together]*	she picks them up like a shot, right away, as if she had
PICKERING:		Beethoven and Brahms or Lehar and Lionel Morickton;[†]
HIGGINS:		been at it all her life.
PICKERING:		though six months ago, she'd never as much as touched a piano—

MRS. HIGGINS: *[putting her fingers in her ears, as they are by this time shouting one another down with an intolerable noise]* Sh—sh—sh—sh! *[They stop]*.

PICKERING: I beg your pardon. *[He draws his chair back apologetically]*.

HIGGINS: Sorry. When Pickering starts shouting nobody can get a word in edgeways.

MRS. HIGGINS: Be quiet, Henry. Colonel Pickering: don't you realize that when Eliza walked into Wimpole Street, something walked in with her?

PICKERING: Her father did. But Henry soon got rid of him.

MRS. HIGGINS: It would have been more to the point if her mother had. But as her mother didn't something else did.

PICKERING: But what?

MRS. HIGGINS: *[unconsciously dating herself by the word]* A problem.

PICKERING: Oh, I see. The problem of how to pass her off as a lady.

HIGGINS: I'll solve that problem. I've half solved it already.

MRS. HIGGINS: No, you two infinitely stupid male creatures: the problem of what is to be done with her afterwards.

HIGGINS: I don't see anything in that. She can go her own way, with all the advantages I have given her.

MRS. HIGGINS: The advantages of that poor woman who was here just now! The manners and habits that disqualify a fine lady from earning her own living without giving her a fine lady's income! Is that what you mean?

PICKERING: *[indulgently, being rather bored]* Oh, that will be all right, Mrs. Higgins. *[He rises to go]*.

HIGGINS: *[rising also]* We'll find her some light employment.

PICKERING: She's happy enough. Don't you worry about her. Good-bye.

[He shakes hands as if he were consoling a frightened child, and makes for the door].

HIGGINS: Anyhow, there's no good bothering now. The thing's done. Good-bye, mother. *[He kisses her, and follows Pickering].*

PICKERING: *[turning for a final consolation]* There are plenty of openings. We'll do what's right. Good-bye.

HIGGINS: *[to Pickering as they go out together]* Let's take her to the Shakespear exhibition at Earls Court.

PICKERING: Yes: let's. Her remarks will be delicious.

HIGGINS: She'll mimic all the people for us when we get home.

PICKERING: Ripping. *[Both are heard laughing as they go downstairs].*

MRS. HIGGINS: *[rises with an impatient bounce, and returns to her work at the writing-table. She sweeps a litter of disarranged papers out of her way; snatches a sheet of paper from her stationery case; and tries resolutely to write. At the third line she gives it up; flings down her pen; grips the table angrily and exclaims]* Oh, men! men!! men!!!

ACT IV

[The Wimpole Street laboratory. Midnight. Nobody in the room. The clock on the mantelpiece strikes twelve. The fire is not alight: it is a summer night.
    Presently Higgins and Pickering are heard on the stairs.]

HIGGINS: *[calling down to Pickering]* I say, Pick: lock up, will you. I shan't be going out again.
PICKERING: Right. Can Mrs. Pearce go to bed? We don't want anything more, do we?
HIGGINS: Lord, no!

[Eliza opens the door and is seen on the lighted landing in opera cloak, brilliant evening dress, and diamonds, with fan, flowers, and all accessories. She comes to the hearth, and switches on the electric lights there. She is tired: her pallor contrasts strongly with her dark eyes and hair; and her expression is almost tragic. She takes off her cloak; puts her fan and flowers on the piano; and sits down on the bench, brooding and silent. Higgins, in evening dress, with overcoat and hat, comes in, carrying a smoking jacket which he has picked up downstairs. He takes off the hat and overcoat; throws them carelessly on the newspaper stand; disposes of his coat in the same way; puts on the smoking jacket; and throws himself wearily into the easy-chair at the hearth. Pickering, similarly attired, comes in. He also takes off his hat and overcoat, and is about to throw them on Higgins's when he hesitates.]

PICKERING: I say: Mrs. Pearce will row if we leave these things lying about in the drawing-room.

HIGGINS: Oh, chuck them over the bannisters into the hall. She'll find them there in the morning and put them away all right. She'll think we were drunk.

PICKERING: We are, slightly. Are there any letters?

HIGGINS: I didn't look. [Pickering takes the overcoats and hats and goes down stairs. Higgins begins half singing half yawning an air from La Fanciulla del Golden West. Suddenly he stops and exclaims] I wonder where the devil my slippers are!

[Eliza looks at him darkly; then rises suddenly and leaves the room.
Higgins yawns again, and resumes his song.
Pickering returns, with the contents of the letter-box in his hand.]

PICKERING: Only circulars, and this coroneted billet-doux for you. [He throws the circulars into the fender, and posts himself on the hearthrug, with his back to the grate].

HIGGINS: [glancing at the billet-doux] Money-lender. [He throws the letter after the circulars].

[Eliza returns with a pair of large down-at-heel slippers. She places them on the carpet before Higgins, and sits as before without a word.]

HIGGINS: [yawning again] Oh Lord! What an evening! What a crew! What a silly tomfoollery! [He raises his shoe to unlace it, and catches sight of the slippers. He stops unlacing and looks at them as if they had appeared there of their own accord]. Oh! they're there, are they?

PICKERING: [stretching himself] Well, I feel a bit tired. It's been a long day. The garden party, a dinner party, and the opera! Rather too much of a good thing. But you've won your bet, Higgins. Eliza did the trick, and something to spare, eh?

HIGGINS: [fervently] Thank God it's over!

[Eliza flinches violently; but they take no notice of her; and she recovers herself and sits stonily as before.]

PICKERING: Were you nervous at the garden party? I was. Eliza didn't seem a bit nervous.

HIGGINS: Oh, she wasn't nervous. I knew she'd be all right. No, it's the strain of putting the job through all these months that has told on me. It was interesting enough at first, while we were at the phonetics; but after that I got deadly sick of it. If I hadn't backed myself to do it I should have chucked the whole thing up two months ago. It was a silly notion: the whole thing has been a bore.

PICKERING: Oh come! the garden party was frightfully exciting. My heart began beating like anything.

HIGGINS: Yes, for the first three minutes. But when I saw we were going to win hands down, I felt like a bear in a cage, hanging about doing nothing. The dinner was worse: sitting gorging there for over an hour, with nobody but a damned fool of a fashionable woman to talk to! I tell you, Pickering, never again for me. No more artificial duchesses. The whole thing has been simple purgatory.

PICKERING: You've never been broken in properly to the social routine. *[Strolling over to the piano]* I rather enjoy dipping into it occasionally myself: it makes me feel young again. Anyhow, it was a great success: an immense success. I was quite frightened once or twice because Eliza was doing it so well. You see, lots of the real people can't do it at all: they're such fools that they think style comes by nature to people in their position; and so they never learn. There's always something professional about doing a thing superlatively well.

HIGGINS: Yes: that's what drives me mad: the silly people don't know their own silly business. *[Rising]* However, it's over and done with; and now I can go to bed at last without dreading tomorrow.

[Eliza's beauty becomes murderous.]

PICKERING: I think I shall turn in too. Still, it's been a great occasion: a triumph for you. Good-night. *[He goes].*

HIGGINS: *[following him]* Good-night. *[Over his shoulder, at the door]* Put out the lights, Eliza; and tell Mrs. Pearce not to make coffee for me in the morning: I'll take tea. *[He goes out].*

[Eliza tries to control herself and feel indifferent as she rises and walks across to the hearth to switch off the lights. By the time she gets there she is on the point of screaming. She sits down in Higgins's chair and holds on hard to the arms. Finally she gives way and flings herself furiously on the floor raging.]

HIGGINS: [in despairing wrath outside] What the devil have I done with my slippers? [He appears at the door].

LIZA: [snatching up the slippers, and hurling them at him one after the other with all her force] There are your slippers. And there. Take your slippers; and may you never have a day's luck with them!

HIGGINS: [astounded] What on earth—! [He comes to her]. What's the matter? Get up. [He pulls her up]. Anything wrong?

LIZA: [breathless] Nothing wrong—with you. I've won your bet for you, haven't I? That's enough for you. I don't matter, I suppose.

HIGGINS: You won my bet! You! Presumptuous insect! I won it. What did you throw those slippers at me for?

LIZA: Because I wanted to smash your face. I'd like to kill you, you selfish brute. Why didn't you leave me where you picked me out of—in the gutter? You thank God it's all over, and that now you can throw me back again there, do you? [She crisps her fingers, frantically].

HIGGINS: [looking at her in cool wonder] The creature is nervous, after all.

LIZA: [gives a suffocated scream of fury, and instinctively darts her nails at his face]!!

HIGGINS: [catching her wrists] Ah! would you? Claws in, you cat. How dare you show your temper to me? Sit down and be quiet. [He throws her roughly into the easy-chair].

LIZA: [crushed by superior strength and weight] What's to become of me? What's to become of me?

HIGGINS: How the devil do I know what's to become of you? What does it matter what becomes of you?

LIZA: You don't care. I know you don't care. You wouldn't care if I was dead. I'm nothing to you—not so much as them slippers.

HIGGINS: [thundering] Those slippers.

LIZA: [with bitter submission] Those slippers. I didn't think it made any difference now.

[A pause. Eliza hopeless and crushed. Higgins a little uneasy.]

HIGGINS: [in his loftiest manner] Why have you begun going on like this? May I ask whether you complain of your treatment here?

LIZA: No.

HIGGINS: Has anybody behaved badly to you? Colonel Pickering? Mrs. Pearce? Any of the servants?

LIZA: No.

HIGGINS: I presume you don't pretend that I have treated you badly.

LIZA: No.

HIGGINS: I am glad to hear it. *[He moderates his tone].* Perhaps you're tired after the strain of the day. Will you have a glass of champagne? *[He moves towards the door].*

LIZA: No. *[Recollecting her manners]* Thank you.

HIGGINS: *[good-humored again]* This has been coming on you for some days. I suppose it was natural for you to be anxious about the garden party. But that's all over now. *[He pats her kindly on the shoulder. She writhes].* There's nothing more to worry about.

LIZA: No. Nothing more for you to worry about. *[She suddenly rises and gets away from him by going to the piano bench, where she sits and hides her face].* Oh God! I wish I was dead.

HIGGINS: *[staring after her in sincere surprise]* Why? in heaven's name, why? *[Reasonably, going to her]* Listen to me, Eliza. All this irritation is purely subjective.

LIZA: I don't understand. I'm too ignorant.

HIGGINS: It's only imagination. Low spirits and nothing else. Nobody's hurting you. Nothing's wrong. You go to bed like a good girl and sleep it off. Have a little cry and say your prayers: that will make you comfortable.

LIZA: I heard your prayers. "Thank God it's all over!"

HIGGINS: *[impatiently]* Well, don't you thank God it's all over? Now you are free and can do what you like.

LIZA: *[pulling herself together in desperation]* What am I fit for? What have you left me fit for? Where am I to go? What am I to do? What's to become of me?

HIGGINS: *[enlightened, but not at all impressed]* Oh, that's what's worrying you, is it? *[He thrusts his hands into his pockets, and walks about in his usual manner, rattling the contents of his pockets, as if condescending to a trivial subject out of pure kindness].* I shouldn't bother about it if I were you. I should imagine you won't have much difficulty in settling yourself, somewhere or other, though I hadn't quite realized that you were going away. *[She looks quickly at him: he does not look at her, but examines the dessert stand on the piano and decides that he will eat an apple].* You might marry, you know. *[He bites a large piece out of the apple, and munches it noisily].* You see, Eliza, all men are not confirmed old bachelors like me and the Colonel. Most men are the marrying sort (poor devils!); and you're not bad-looking; it's quite a pleasure to look at you sometimes—not now, of course, because you're crying and looking as ugly as the very devil; but when you're all right and quite yourself, you're what I should call attractive. That is, to the people in the marrying line, you understand. You go to bed and have a good nice rest; and then get up and look at yourself in the glass; and you won't feel so cheap.

[*Eliza again looks at him, speechless, and does not stir.*

The look is quite lost on him: he eats his apple with a dreamy expression of happiness, as it is quite a good one.]

HIGGINS: [*a genial afterthought occurring to him*] I daresay my mother could find some chap or other who would do very well.

LIZA: We were above that at the corner of Tottenham Court Road.

HIGGINS: [*waking up*] What do you mean?

LIZA: I sold flowers. I didn't sell myself. Now you've made a lady of me I'm not fit to sell anything else. I wish you'd left me where you found me.

HIGGINS: [*slinging the core of the apple decisively into the grate*] Tosh, Eliza. Don't you insult human relations by dragging all this cant about buying and selling into it. You needn't marry the fellow if you don't like him.

LIZA: What else am I to do?

HIGGINS: Oh, lots of things. What about your old idea of a florist's shop? Pickering could set you up in one: he's lots of money. [*Chuckling*] He'll have to pay for all those togs you have been wearing today; and that, with the hire of the jewellery, will make a big hole in two hundred pounds. Why, six months ago you would have thought it the millennium to have a flower shop of your own. Come! you'll be all right. I must clear off to bed: I'm devilish sleepy. By the way, I came down for something: I forget what it was.

LIZA: Your slippers.

HIGGINS: Oh yes, of course. You shied them at me. [*He picks them up, and is going out when she rises and speaks to him*].

LIZA: Before you go, sir—

HIGGINS: [*dropping the slippers in his surprise at her calling him sir*] Eh?

LIZA: Do my clothes belong to me or to Colonel Pickering?

HIGGINS: [*coming back into the room as if her question were the very climax of unreason*] What the devil use would they be to Pickering?

LIZA: He might want them for the next girl you pick up to experiment on.

HIGGINS: *[shocked and hurt]* Is that the way you feel towards us?

LIZA: I don't want to hear anything more about that. All I want to know is whether anything belongs to me. My own clothes were burnt.

HIGGINS: But what does it matter? Why need you start bothering about that in the middle of the night?

LIZA: I want to know what I may take away with me. I don't want to be accused of stealing.

HIGGINS: *[now deeply wounded]* Stealing! You shouldn't have said that, Eliza. That shows a want of feeling.

LIZA: I'm sorry. I'm only a common ignorant girl; and in my station I have to be careful. There can't be any feelings between the like of you and the like of me. Please will you tell me what belongs to me and what doesn't?

HIGGINS: *[very sulky]* You may take the whole damned houseful if you like. Except the jewels. They're hired. Will that satisfy you? *[He turns on his heel and is about to go in extreme dudgeon]*.

LIZA: *[drinking in his emotion like nectar, and nagging him to provoke a further supply]* Stop, please. *[She takes off her jewels]*. Will you take these to your room and keep them safe? I don't want to run the risk of their being missing.

HIGGINS: *[furious]* Hand them over. *[She puts them into his hands]*. If these belonged to me instead of to the jeweler, I'd ram them down your ungrateful throat. *[He perfunctorily thrusts them into his pockets, unconsciously decorating himself with the protruding ends of the chains]*.

LIZA: *[taking a ring off]* This ring isn't the jeweler's: it's the one you bought me in Brighton. I don't want it now. *[Higgins dashes the ring violently into the fireplace, and turns on her so threateningly that she crouches over the piano with her hands over her face, and exclaims]* Don't you hit me.

HIGGINS: Hit you! You infamous creature, how dare you accuse me of such a thing? It is you who have hit me. You have wounded me to the heart.

LIZA: *[thrilling with hidden joy]* I'm glad. I've got a little of my own back, anyhow.

HIGGINS: *[with dignity, in his finest professional style]* You have caused me to lose my temper: a thing that has hardly ever happened to me before. I prefer to say nothing more tonight. I am going to bed.

LIZA: *[pertly]* You'd better leave a note for Mrs. Pearce about the coffee; for she won't be told by me.

HIGGINS: *[formally]* Damn Mrs. Pearce; and damn the coffee; and damn you; and damn my own folly in having lavished hard-earned knowledge and the treasure of my regard and intimacy on a heartless guttersnipe. *[He goes out with impressive decorum, and spoils it by slamming the door savagely].*

[Eliza smiles for the first time; expresses her feelings by a wild pantomime in which an imitation of Higgins's exit is confused with her own triumph; and finally goes down on her knees on the hearthrug to look for the ring.]

ACT V

[*Mrs. Higgins's drawing room. She is at her writing-table as before. The parlor-maid comes in.*]

THE PARLOR-MAID: [*at the door*]   Mr. Henry, mam, is downstairs with Colonel Pickering.

MRS. HIGGINS: Well, show them up.

THE PARLOR-MAID: They're using the telephone, mam. Telephoning to the police, I think.

MRS. HIGGINS: What!

THE PARLOR-MAID: [*coming further in and lowering her voice*] Mr. Henry's in a state, mam. I thought I'd better tell you.

MRS. HIGGINS: If you had told me that Mr. Henry was not in a state it would have been more surprising. Tell them to come up when they've finished with the police. I suppose he's lost something.

THE PARLOR-MAID: Yes, mam [*going*].

MRS. HIGGINS: Go upstairs and tell Miss Doolittle that Mr. Henry and the Colonel are here. Ask her not to come down till I send for her.

THE PARLOR-MAID: Yes, mam.

[*Higgins bursts in. He is, as the parlor-maid has said, in a state.*]

HIGGINS: Look here, mother: here's a confounded thing!

MRS. HIGGINS: Yes, dear. Good-morning. [*He checks his impatience and kisses her, whilst the parlor-maid goes out].* What is it?

HIGGINS: Eliza's bolted.

MRS. HIGGINS: *[calmly continuing her writing]* You must have frightened her.

HIGGINS: Frightened her! nonsense! She was left last night, as usual, to turn out the lights and all that; and instead of going to bed she changed her clothes and went right off: her bed wasn't slept in. She came in a cab for her things before seven this morning; and that fool Mrs. Pearce let her have them without telling me a word about it. What am I to do?

MRS. HIGGINS: Do without, I'm afraid, Henry. The girl has a perfect right to leave if she chooses.

HIGGINS: *[wandering distractedly across the room]* But I can't find anything. I don't know what appointments I've got. I'm—*[Pickering comes in. Mrs. Higgins puts down her pen and turns away from the writing-table].*

PICKERING: *[shaking hands]* Good-morning, Mrs. Higgins. Has Henry told you? *[He sits down on the ottoman].*

HIGGINS: What does that ass of an inspector say? Have you offered a reward?

MRS. HIGGINS: *[rising in indignant amazement]* You don't mean to say you have set the police after Eliza?

HIGGINS: Of course. What are the police for? What else could we do? *[He sits in the Elizabethan chair].*

PICKERING: The inspector made a lot of difficulties. I really think he suspected us of some improper purpose.

MRS. HIGGINS: Well, of course he did. What right have you to go to the police and give the girl's name as if she were a thief, or a lost umbrella, or something? Really! *[She sits down again, deeply vexed].*

HIGGINS: But we want to find her.

PICKERING: We can't let her go like this, you know, Mrs. Higgins. What were we to do?

MRS. HIGGINS: You have no more sense, either of you, than two children. Why—

[The parlor-maid comes in and breaks off the conversation.]

THE PARLOR-MAID: Mr, Henry: a gentleman wants to see you very particular. He's been sent on from Wimpole Street.

HIGGINS: Oh, bother! I can't see anyone now. Who is it?

THE PARLOR-MAID: A Mr. Doolittle, Sir.

PICKERING: Doolittle! Do you mean the dustman?

THE PARLOR-MAID: Dustman! Oh no, sir: a gentleman.

HIGGINS: *[springing up excitedly]* By George, Pick, it's some relative of hers that she's gone to. Somebody we know nothing about. *[To the parlor-maid]* Send him up, quick.

THE PARLOR-MAID: Yes, Sir. *[She goes]*.

HIGGINS: *[eagerly, going to his mother]* Genteel relatives! now we shall hear something. *[He sits down in the Chippendale chair]*.

MRS. HIGGINS: Do you know any of her people?

PICKERING: Only her father: the fellow we told you about.

THE PARLOR-MAID: *[announcing]* Mr. Doolittle. *[She withdraws]*.

[Doolittle enters. He is brilliantly dressed in a new fashionable frock-coat, with white waistcoat and grey trousers. A flower in his buttonhole, a dazzling silk hat, and patent leather shoes complete the effect. He is too concerned with the business he has come on to notice Mrs. Higgins. He walks straight to Higgins, and accosts him with vehement reproach.]

DOOLITTLE: *[indicating his own person]* See here! Do you see this? You done this.

HIGGINS: Done what, man?

DOOLITTLE: This, I tell you. Look at it. Look at this hat. Look at this coat.

PICKERING: Has Eliza been buying you clothes?

DOOLITTLE: Eliza! not she. Not half. Why would she buy me clothes?

MRS. HIGGINS: Good-morning, Mr. Doolittle. Won't you sit down?

DOOLITTLE: *[taken aback as he becomes conscious that he has forgotten his hostess]* Asking your pardon, ma'am. *[He approaches her and shakes her proffered hand]*. Thank you. *[He sits down on the ottoman, on Pickering's right]*. I am that full of what has happened to me that I can't think of anything else.

HIGGINS: What the dickens has happened to you?

DOOLITTLE: I shouldn't mind if it had only happened to me: anything might happen to anybody and nobody to blame but Providence, as you might say. But this is something that you done to me: yes, you, Henry Higgins.

HIGGINS: Have you found Eliza? That's the point.

DOOLITTLE: Have you lost her?

HIGGINS: Yes.

DOOLITTLE: You have all the luck, you have. I ain't found her; but she'll find me quick enough now after what you done to me.

MRS. HIGGINS: But what has my son done to you, Mr. Doolittle?

DOOLITTLE: Done to me! Ruined me. Destroyed my happiness. Tied me up and delivered me into the hands of middle class morality.

HIGGINS: *[rising intolerantly and standing over Doolittle]* You're raving. You're drunk. You're mad. I gave you five pounds. After that I had two conversations with you, at half-a-crown an hour. I've never seen you since.

DOOLITTLE: Oh! Drunk! am I? Mad! am I? Tell me this. Did you or did you not write a letter to an old blighter in America that was giving five millions to found Moral Reform Societies† all over the world, and that wanted you to invent a universal language for him?

HIGGINS: What! Ezra D. Wannafeller! He's dead. *[He sits down again carelessly]*.

DOOLITTLE: Yes: he's dead; and I'm done for. Now did you or did you not write a letter to him to say that the most original moralist at present in England, to the best of your knowledge, was Alfred Doolittle, a common dustman.

HIGGINS: Oh, after your last visit I remember making some silly joke of the kind.

DOOLITTLE: Ah! you may well call it a silly joke. It put the lid on me right enough. Just give him the chance he wanted to show that Americans is not like us: that they recognize and respect merit in every class of life, however humble. Them words is in his blooming will, in which, Henry Higgins, thanks to your silly joking, he leaves me a share in his Pre-digested Cheese Trust worth three thousand a year on condition that I lecture for his Wannafeller Moral Reform World League as often as they ask me up to six times a year.

HIGGINS: The devil he does! Whew! *[Brightening suddenly]* What a lark!

PICKERING: A safe thing for you, Doolittle. They won't ask you twice.

DOOLITTLE: It ain't the lecturing I mind. I'll lecture them blue in the face, I will, and not turn a hair. It's making a gentleman of me that I object to. Who asked him to make a gentleman of me? I was happy. I was free. I touched pretty nigh everybody for money when I wanted it, same as I touched you, Henry Higgins. Now I am worrited; tied neck and heels; and everybody touches me for money. It's a fine thing for you, says my solicitor. Is it? says I. You mean it's a good thing for you, I says. When I was a poor man and had a solicitor once when they found a pram in the dust cart, he got me off, and got shut of me and got me shut of him as quick as he could. Same with the doctors: used to shove me out of the hospital before I could hardly stand on my legs, and nothing to pay. Now they finds out that I'm not a healthy man and can't live unless they looks after me twice a day. In the house I'm not let do a hand's turn for myself: somebody else must do it and touch me for it. A year ago I hadn't a relative in the world except two or three that wouldn't speak to me. Now I've fifty, and not a decent week's wages among the lot of them. I have to live for others and not for myself: that's middle class morality. You talk of losing Eliza. Don't you be anxious: I bet she's on my doorstep by this: she that could support herself easy by selling flowers if I wasn't respectable. And the next one to touch me will be you, Henry Higgins. I'll have to learn to speak middle class language from you, instead of speaking proper English. That's where you'll come in; and I daresay that's what you done it for.

MRS. HIGGINS: But, my dear Mr. Doolittle, you need not suffer all this if you are really in earnest. Nobody can force you to accept this bequest. You can repudiate it. Isn't that so, Colonel Pickering?

PICKERING: I believe so.

DOOLITTLE: [softening his manner in deference to her sex] That's the tragedy of it, ma'am. It's easy to say chuck it; but I haven't the nerve. Which one of us has? We're all intimidated. Intimidated, ma'am: that's what we are. What is there for me if I chuck it but the workhouse in my old age? I have to dye my hair already to keep my job as a dustman. If I was one of the deserving poor, and had put by a bit, I could chuck it; but then why should I, acause the deserving poor might as well be millionaires for all the happiness they ever has. They don't know what happiness is. But I, as one of the undeserving poor, have nothing between me and the pauper's uniform but this here blasted three thousand a year that shoves me into the middle class. (Excuse the expression, ma'am: you'd use it yourself if you had my provocation). They've got you every way you turn: it's a choice between the Skilly of the workhouse and the Char Bydis of the middle class; and I haven't the nerve for the workhouse. Intimidated: that's what I am. Broke. Bought up. Happier men than me will call for my dust, and touch me for their tip; and I'll look on helpless, and envy them. And that's what your son has brought me to. [He is overcome by emotion].

MRS. HIGGINS: Well, I'm very glad you're not going to do anything foolish, Mr. Doolittle. For this solves the problem of Eliza's future. You can provide for her now.

DOOLITTLE: [with melancholy resignation] Yes, ma'am; I'm expected to provide for everyone now, out of three thousand a year.

HIGGINS: [jumping up] Nonsense! he can't provide for her. He shan't provide for her. She doesn't belong to him. I paid him five pounds for her. Doolittle: either you're an honest man or a rogue.

DOOLITTLE: [tolerantly] A little of both, Henry, like the rest of us: a little of both.

HIGGINS: Well, you took that money for the girl; and you have no right to take her as well.

MRS. HIGGINS: Henry: don't be absurd. If you really want to know where Eliza is, she is upstairs.

HIGGINS: [amazed] Upstairs!!! Then I shall jolly soon fetch her downstairs. [He makes resolutely for the door].

MRS. HIGGINS: [rising and following him] Be quiet, Henry. Sit down.

HIGGINS: I—

MRS. HIGGINS: Sit down, dear; and listen to me.

HIGGINS: Oh very well, very well, very well. [He throws himself ungraciously on the ottoman, with his face towards the windows]. But I think you might have told me this half an hour ago.

MRS. HIGGINS: Eliza came to me this morning. She passed the night partly walking about in a rage, partly trying to throw herself into the river and being afraid to, and partly in the Carlton Hotel. She told me of the brutal way you two treated her.

HIGGINS: [bounding up again] What!

PICKERING: [rising also] My dear Mrs. Higgins, she's been telling you stories. We didn't treat her brutally. We hardly said a word to her; and we parted on particularly good terms. [Turning on Higgins]. Higgins did you bully her after I went to bed?

HIGGINS: Just the other way about. She threw my slippers in my face. She behaved in the most outrageous way. I never gave her the slightest provocation. The slippers came bang into my face the moment I entered the room—before I had uttered a word. And used perfectly awful language.

PICKERING: [astonished] But why? What did we do to her?

MRS. HIGGINS: I think I know pretty well what you did. The girl is naturally rather affectionate, I think. Isn't she, Mr. Doolittle?

DOOLITTLE: Very tender-hearted, ma'am. Takes after me.

MRS. HIGGINS: Just so. She had become attached to you both. She worked very hard for you, Henry! I don't think you quite realize what anything in the nature of brain work means to a girl like that. Well, it seems that when the great day of trial came, and she did this wonderful thing for you without making a single mistake, you two sat there and never said a word to her, but talked together of how glad you were that it was all over and how you had been bored with the whole thing. And then you were surprised because she threw your slippers at you! *I* should have thrown the fire-irons at you.

HIGGINS: We said nothing except that we were tired and wanted to go to bed. Did we, Pick?

PICKERING: [shrugging his shoulders] That was all.

MRS. HIGGINS: [ironically] Quite sure?

PICKERING: Absolutely. Really, that was all.

MRS. HIGGINS: You didn't thank her, or pet her, or admire her, or tell her how splendid she'd been.

HIGGINS: [impatiently] But she knew all about that. We didn't make speeches to her, if that's what you mean.

PICKERING: [conscience stricken] Perhaps we were a little inconsiderate. Is she very angry?

MRS. HIGGINS: [returning to her place at the writing-table] Well, I'm afraid she won't go back to Wimpole Street, especially now that Mr. Doolittle is able to keep up the position you have thrust on her; but she says she is quite willing to meet you on friendly terms and to let bygones be bygones.

HIGGINS: [furious] Is she, by George? Ho!

MRS. HIGGINS: If you promise to behave yourself, Henry, I'll ask her to come down. If not, go home; for you have taken up quite enough of my time.

HIGGINS: Oh, all right. Very well. Pick: you behave yourself. Let us put on our best Sunday manners for this creature that we picked out of the mud. [He flings himself sulkily into the Elizabethan chair].

DOOLITTLE: [remonstrating] Now, now, Henry Higgins! have some consideration for my feelings as a middle class man.

MRS. HIGGINS: Remember your promise, Henry. [She presses the bell-button on the writing-table]. Mr. Doolittle: will you be so good as to step out on the balcony for a moment. I don't want Eliza to have the shock of your news until she has made it up with these two gentlemen. Would you mind?

DOOLITTLE: As you wish, lady. Anything to help Henry to keep her off my hands. *[He disappears through the window].*

[The parlor-maid answers the bell. Pickering sits down in Doolittle's place.]

MRS. HIGGINS: Ask Miss Doolittle to come down, please.
THE PARLOR-MAID: Yes, mam. *[She goes out].*
MRS. HIGGINS: Now, Henry: be good.
HIGGINS: I am behaving myself perfectly.
PICKERING: He is doing his best, Mrs. Higgins.

[A pause. Higgins throws back his head; stretches out his legs; and begins to whistle.]

MRS. HIGGINS: Henry, dearest, you don't look at all nice in that attitude.
HIGGINS: *[pulling himself together]* I was not trying to look nice, mother.
MRS. HIGGINS: It doesn't matter, dear. I only wanted to make you speak.
HIGGINS: Why?
MRS. HIGGINS: Because you can't speak and whistle at the same time.

[Higgins groans. Another very trying pause.]

HIGGINS: *[springing up, out of patience]* Where the devil is that girl? Are we to wait here all day?

[Eliza enters, sunny, self-possessed, and giving a staggeringly convincing exhibition of ease of manner. She carries a little work-basket, and is very much at home. Pickering is too much taken aback to rise.]

LIZA: How do you do, Professor Higgins? Are you quite well?
HIGGINS: *[choking]* Am I—*[He can say no more].*
LIZA: But of course you are: you are never ill. So glad to see you again, Colonel Pickering. *[He rises hastily; and they shake hands].* Quite chilly this morning, isn't it? *[She sits down on his left. He sits beside her].*
HIGGINS: Don't you dare try this game on me. I taught it to you; and it doesn't take me in. Get up and come home; and don't be a fool.

[Eliza takes a piece of needlework from her basket, and begins to stitch at it, without taking the least notice of this outburst.]

MRS. HIGGINS: Very nicely put, indeed, Henry. No woman could resist such an invitation.

HIGGINS: You let her alone, mother. Let her speak for herself. You will jolly soon see whether she has an idea that I haven't put into her head or a word that I haven't put into her mouth. I tell you I have created this thing out of the squashed cabbage leaves of Covent Garden; and now she pretends to play the fine lady with me.

MRS. HIGGINS: *[placidly]* Yes, dear; but you'll sit down, won't you?

[Higgins sits down again, savagely].

LIZA: *[to Pickering, taking no apparent notice of Higgins, and working away deftly]* Will you drop me altogether now that the experiment is over, Colonel Pickering?

PICKERING: Oh don't. You mustn't think of it as an experiment. It shocks me, somehow.

LIZA: Oh, I'm only a squashed cabbage leaf.

PICKERING: *[impulsively]* No.

LIZA: *[continuing quietly]*—but I owe so much to you that I should be very unhappy if you forgot me.

PICKERING: It's very kind of you to say so, Miss Doolittle.

LIZA: It's not because you paid for my dresses. I know you are generous to everybody with money. But it was from you that I learnt really nice manners; and that is what makes one a lady, isn't it? You see it was so very difficult for me with the example of Professor Higgins always before me. I was brought up to be just like him, unable to control myself, and using bad language on the slightest provocation. And I should never have known that ladies and gentlemen didn't behave like that if you hadn't been there.

HIGGINS: Well!!

PICKERING: Oh, that's only his way, you know. He doesn't mean it.

LIZA: Oh, I didn't mean it either, when I was a flower girl. It was only my way. But you see I did it; and that's what makes the difference after all.

PICKERING: No doubt. Still, he taught you to speak; and I couldn't have done that, you know.

LIZA: *[trivially]* Of course: that is his profession.

HIGGINS: Damnation!

LIZA: *[continuing]* It was just like learning to dance in the fashionable way: there was nothing more than that in it. But do you know what began my real education?

PICKERING: What?

LIZA: *[stopping her work for a moment]* Your calling me Miss Doolittle that day when I first came to Wimpole Street. That was the beginning of self-respect for me. *[She resumes her stitching].* And there were a hundred little things you never noticed, because they came naturally to you. Things about standing up and taking off your hat and opening doors—

PICKERING: Oh, that was nothing.

LIZA: Yes: things that showed you thought and felt about me as if I were something better than a scullerymaid; though of course I know you would have been just the same to a scullery-maid if she had been let in the drawing-room. You never took off your boots in the dining room when I was there.

PICKERING: You mustn't mind that. Higgins takes off his boots all over the place.

LIZA: I know. I am not blaming him. It is his way, isn't it? But it made such a difference to me that you didn't do it. You see, really and truly, apart from the things anyone can pick up (the dressing and the proper way of speaking, and so on), the difference between a lady and a flower girl is not how she behaves, but how she's treated. I shall always be a flower girl to Professor Higgins, because he always treats me as a flower girl, and always will; but I know I can be a lady to you, because you always treat me as a lady, and always will.

MRS. HIGGINS: Please don't grind your teeth, Henry.

PICKERING: Well, this is really very nice of you, Miss Doolittle.

LIZA: I should like you to call me Eliza, now, if you would.

PICKERING: Thank you. Eliza, of course.

LIZA: And I should like Professor Higgins to call me Miss Doolittle.

HIGGINS: I'll see you damned first.

MRS. HIGGINS: Henry! Henry!

PICKERING: *[laughing]* Why don't you slang back at him? Don't stand it. It would do him a lot of good.

LIZA: I can't. I could have done it once; but now I can't go back to it. Last night, when I was wandering about, a girl spoke to me; and I tried to get back into the old way with her; but it was no use. You told me, you know, that when a child is brought to a foreign country, it picks up the language in a few weeks, and forgets its own. Well, I am a child in your country. I have forgotten my own language, and can speak nothing but yours. That's the real break-off with the corner of Tottenham Court Road. Leaving Wimpole Street finishes it.

PICKERING: *[much alarmed]* Oh! but you're coming back to Wimpole Street, aren't you? You'll forgive Higgins?

HIGGINS: *[rising]* Forgive! Will she, by George! Let her go. Let her find out how she can get on without us. She will relapse into the gutter in three weeks without me at her elbow.

[Doolittle appears at the centre window. With a look of dignified reproach at Higgins, he comes slowly and silently to his daughter, who, with her back to the window, is unconscious of his approach.]

PICKERING: He's incorrigible, Eliza. You won't relapse, will you?

LIZA: No: Not now. Never again. I have learnt my lesson. I don't believe I could utter one of the old sounds if I tried. *[Doolittle touches her on her left shoulder. She drops her work, losing her self-possession utterly at the spectacle of her father's splendor]* A—a—a—a—a—ah—ow—ooh!

HIGGINS:*[with a crow of triumph]* Aha! Just so. A—a—a—a—ahowooh! A—a—a—a—ahowooh ! A—a—a—a—ahowooh! Victory! Victory! *[He throws himself on the divan, folding his arms, and spraddling arrogantly]*.

DOOLITTLE. Can you blame the girl? Don't look at me like that, Eliza. It ain't my fault. I've come into money.

LIZA: You must have touched a millionaire this time, dad.

DOOLITTLE: I have. But I'm dressed something special today. I'm going to St. George's, Hanover Square. Your stepmother is going to marry me.

LIZA: *[angrily]* You're going to let yourself down to marry that low common woman!

PICKERING: *[quietly]* He ought to, Eliza. *[To Doolittle]* Why has she changed her mind?

DOOLITTLE: *[sadly]* Intimidated, Governor. Intimidated. Middle class morality claims its victim. Won't you put on your hat, Liza, and come and see me turned off?

LIZA: If the Colonel says I must, I—I'll *[almost sobbing]* I'll demean myself. And get insulted for my pains, like enough.

DOOLITTLE: Don't be afraid: she never comes to words with anyone now, poor woman! respectability has broke all the spirit out of her.

PICKERING: *[squeezing Eliza's elbow gently]* Be kind to them, Eliza. Make the best of it.

LIZA: *[forcing a little smile for him through her vexation]* Oh well, just to show there's no ill feeling. I'll be back in a moment. *[She goes out]*.

DOOLITTLE: *[sitting down beside Pickering]* I feel uncommon nervous about the ceremony, Colonel. I wish you'd come and see me through it.

PICKERING: But you've been through it before, man. You were married to Eliza's mother.

DOOLITTLE: Who told you that, Colonel?

PICKERING: Well, nobody told me. But I concluded naturally—

DOOLITTLE: No: that ain't the natural way, Colonel: it's only the middle class way. My way was always the undeserving way. But don't say nothing to Eliza. She don't know: I always had a delicacy about telling her.

PICKERING: Quite right. We'll leave it so, if you don't mind.

DOOLITTLE: And you'll come to the church, Colonel, and put me through straight?

PICKERING: With pleasure. As far as a bachelor can.

MRS. HIGGINS: May I come, Mr. Doolittle? I should be very sorry to miss your wedding.

DOOLITTLE: I should indeed be honored by your condescension, ma'am; and my poor old woman would take it as a tremenjous compliment. She's been very low, thinking of the happy days that are no more.

MRS. HIGGINS: *[rising]* I'll order the carriage and get ready. *[The men rise, except Higgins]*. I shan't be more than fifteen minutes. *[As she goes to the door Eliza comes in, hatted and buttoning her gloves]*. I'm going to the church to see your father married, Eliza. You had better come in the brougham with me. Colonel Pickering can go on with the bridegroom.

[Mrs. Higgins goes out. Eliza comes to the middle of the room between the centre window and the ottoman. Pickering joins her.]

DOOLITTLE: Bridegroom! What a word! It makes a man realize his position, somehow. *[He takes up his hat and goes towards the door]*.

PICKERING: Before I go, Eliza, do forgive him and come back to us.

LIZA: I don't think papa would allow me. Would you, dad?

DOOLITTLE: *[sad but magnanimous]* They played you off very cunning, Eliza, them two sportsmen. If it had been only one of them, you could have nailed him. But you see, there was two; and one of them chaperoned the other, as you might say. *[To Pickering]* It was artful of you, Colonel; but I bear no malice: I should have done the same myself. I been the victim of one woman after another all my life; and I don't grudge you two getting the better of Eliza. I shan't interfere. It's time for us to go, Colonel. So long, Henry. See you in St. George's, Eliza. *[He goes out].*

PICKERING: *[coaxing]* Do stay with us, Eliza. *[He follows Doolittle].*

[Eliza goes out on the balcony to avoid being alone with Higgins. He rises and joins her there. She immediately comes back into the room and makes for the door; but he goes along the balcony quickly and gets his back to the door before she reaches it.]

HIGGINS: Well, Eliza, you've had a bit of your own back, as you call it. Have you had enough? and are you going to be reasonable? Or do you want any more?

LIZA: You want me back only to pick up your slippers and put up with your tempers and fetch and carry for you.

HIGGINS: I haven't said I wanted you back at all.

LIZA: Oh, indeed. Then what are we talking about?

HIGGINS: About you, not about me. If you come back I shall treat you just as I have always treated you. I can't change my nature; and I don't intend to change my manners. My manners are exactly the same as Colonel Pickering's.

LIZA: That's not true. He treats a flower girl as if she was a duchess.

HIGGINS: And I treat a duchess as if she was a flower girl.

LIZA: I see. *[She turns away composedly, and sits on the ottoman, facing the window]*. The same to everybody.

HIGGINS: Just so.

LIZA: Like father.

HIGGINS: *[grinning, a little taken down]* Without accepting the comparison at all points, Eliza, it's quite true that your father is not a snob, and that he will be quite at home in any station of life to which his eccentric destiny may call him. *[Seriously]* The great secret, Eliza, is not having bad manners or good manners or any other particular sort of manners, but having the same manner for all human souls: in short, behaving as if you were in Heaven, where there are no third-class carriages, and one soul is as good as another.

LIZA: Amen. You are a born preacher.

HIGGINS: *[irritated]* The question is not whether I treat you rudely, but whether you ever heard me treat anyone else better.

LIZA: *[with sudden sincerity]* I don't care how you treat me. I don't mind your swearing at me. I don't mind a black eye: I've had one before this. But *[standing up and facing him]* I won't be passed over.

HIGGINS: Then get out of my way; for I won't stop for you. You talk about me as if I were a motor bus.

LIZA: So you are a motor bus: all bounce and go, and no consideration for anyone. But I can do without you: don't think I can't.

HIGGINS: I know you can. I told you you could.

LIZA: *[wounded, getting away from him to the other side of the ottoman with her face to the hearth]* I know you did, you brute. You wanted to get rid of me.

HIGGINS: Liar.

LIZA: Thank you. *[She sits down with dignity]*.

HIGGINS: You never asked yourself, I suppose, whether *I* could do without you.

LIZA: *[earnestly]* Don't you try to get round me. You'll have to do without me.

HIGGINS: *[arrogant]* I can do without anybody. I have my own soul: my own spark of divine fire. But *[with sudden humility]* I shall miss you, Eliza. *[He sits down near her on the ottoman]*. I have learnt something from your idiotic notions: I confess that humbly and gratefully. And I have grown accustomed to your voice and appearance. I like them, rather.

LIZA: Well, you have both of them on your gramophone and in your book of photographs. When you feel lonely without me, you can turn the machine on. It's got no feelings to hurt.

HIGGINS: I can't turn your soul on. Leave me those feelings; and you can take away the voice and the face. They are not you.

LIZA: Oh, you are a devil. You can twist the heart in a girl as easy as some could twist her arms to hurt her. Mrs. Pearce warned me. Time and again she has wanted to leave you; and you always got round her at the last minute. And you don't care a bit for her. And you don't care a bit for me.

HIGGINS: I care for life, for humanity; and you are a part of it that has come my way and been built into my house. What more can you or anyone ask?

LIZA: I won't care for anybody that doesn't care for me.

HIGGINS: Commercial principles, Eliza. Like *[reproducing her Covent Garden pronunciation with professional exactness]* s'yollin voylets *[selling violets]*, isn't it?

LIZA: Don't sneer at me. It's mean to sneer at me.

HIGGINS: I have never sneered in my life. Sneering doesn't become either the human face or the human soul. I am expressing my righteous contempt for Commercialism. I don't and won't trade in affection. You call me a brute because you couldn't buy a claim on me by fetching my slippers and finding my spectacles. You were a fool: I think a woman fetching a man's slippers is a disgusting sight: did I ever fetch your slippers? I think a good deal more of you for throwing them in my face. No use slaving for me and then saying you want to be cared for: who cares for a slave? If you come back, come back for the sake of good fellowship; for you'll get nothing else. You've had a thousand times as much out of me as I have out of you; and if you dare to set up your little dog's tricks of fetching and carrying slippers against my creation of a Duchess Eliza, I'll slam the door in your silly face.

LIZA: What did you do it for if you didn't care for me?

HIGGINS: [heartily] Why, because it was my job.

LIZA: You never thought of the trouble it would make for me.

HIGGINS: Would the world ever have been made if its maker had been afraid of making trouble? Making life means making trouble. There's only one way of escaping trouble; and that's killing things. Cowards, you notice, are always shrieking to have troublesome people killed.

LIZA: I'm no preacher: I don't notice things like that. I notice that you don't notice me.

HIGGINS: [jumping up and walking about intolerantly] Eliza: you're an idiot. I waste the treasures of my Miltonic mind by spreading them before you. Once for all, understand that I go my way and do my work without caring twopence what happens to either of us. I am not intimidated, like your father and your stepmother. So you can come back or go to the devil: which you please.

LIZA: What am I to come back for?

HIGGINS: [bouncing up on his knees on the ottoman and leaning over it to her] For the fun of it. That's why I took you on.

LIZA: [with averted face] And you may throw me out tomorrow if I don't do everything you want me to?

HIGGINS: Yes; and you may walk out tomorrow if I don't do everything you want me to.

LIZA: And live with my stepmother?

HIGGINS: Yes, or sell flowers.

LIZA: Oh! if I only could go back to my flower basket! I should be independent of both you and father and all the world! Why did you take my independence from me? Why did I give it up? I'm a slave now, for all my fine clothes.

HIGGINS: Not a bit. I'll adopt you as my daughter and settle money on you if you like. Or would you rather marry Pickering?

LIZA: *[looking fiercely round at him]* I wouldn't marry you if you asked me; and you're nearer my age than what he is.

HIGGINS: *[gently]* Than he is: not "than what he is."

LIZA: *[losing her temper and rising]* I'll talk as I like. You're not my teacher now.

HIGGINS: *[reflectively]* I don't suppose Pickering would, though. He's as confirmed an old bachelor as I am.

LIZA: That's not what I want; and don't you think it. I've always had chaps enough wanting me that way. Freddy Hill writes to me twice and three times a day, sheets and sheets.

HIGGINS: *[disagreeably surprised]* Damn his impudence! *[He recoils and finds himself sitting on his heels].*

LIZA: He has a right to if he likes, poor lad. And he does love me.

HIGGINS: *[getting off the ottoman]* You have no right to encourage him.

LIZA: Every girl has a right to be loved.

HIGGINS: What! By fools like that?

LIZA: Freddy's not a fool. And if he's weak and poor and wants me, may be he'd make me happier than my betters that bully me and don't want me.

HIGGINS: Can he make anything of you? That's the point.

LIZA: Perhaps I could make something of him. But I never thought of us making anything of one another; and you never think of anything else. I only want to be natural.

HIGGINS: In short, you want me to be as infatuated about you as Freddy? Is that it?

LIZA: No I don't. That's not the sort of feeling I want from you. And don't you be too sure of yourself or of me. I could have been a bad girl if I'd liked. I've seen more of some things than you, for all your learning. Girls like me can drag gentlemen down to make love to them easy enough. And they wish each other dead the next minute.

HIGGINS: Of course they do. Then what in thunder are we quarrelling about?

LIZA: *[much troubled]* I want a little kindness. I know I'm a common igno- rant girl, and you a book-learned gentleman; but I'm not dirt under your feet. What I done *[correcting herself]* what I did was not for the dresses and the taxis: I did it because we were pleasant together and I come—came—to care for you; not to want you to make love to me, and not forgetting the difference between us, but more friendly like.

HIGGINS: Well, of course. That's just how I feel. And how Pickering feels. Eliza: you're a fool.

LIZA: That's not a proper answer to give me *[she sinks on the chair at the writing-table in tears]*.

HIGGINS: It's all you'll get until you stop being a common idiot. If you're going to be a lady, you'll have to give up feeling neglected if the men you know don't spend half their time snivelling over you and the other half giving you black eyes. If you can't stand the coldness of my sort of life, and the strain of it, go back to the gutter. Work til you are more a brute than a human being; and then cuddle and squabble and drink til you fall asleep. Oh, it's a fine life, the life of the gutter. It's real: it's warm: it's violent: you can feel it through the thickest skin: you can taste it and smell it without any training or any work. Not like Science and Literature and Classical Music and Philosophy and Art. You find me cold, unfeeling, selfish, don't you? Very well: be off with you to the sort of people you like. Marry some sentimental hog or other with lots of money, and a thick pair of lips to kiss you with and a thick pair of boots to kick you with. If you can't appreciate what you've got, you'd better get what you can appreciate.

LIZA: *[desperate]* Oh, you are a cruel tyrant. I can't talk to you: you turn everything against me: I'm always in the wrong. But you know very well all the time that you're nothing but a bully. You know I can't go back to the gutter, as you call it, and that I have no real friends in the world but you and the Colonel. You know well I couldn't bear to live with a low common man after you two; and it's wicked and cruel of you to insult me by pretending I could. You think I must go back to Wimpole Street because I have nowhere else to go but father's. But don't you be too sure that you have me under your feet to be trampled on and talked down. I'll marry Freddy, I will, as soon as he's able to support me.

HIGGINS: *[sitting down beside her]* Rubbish! you shall marry an ambassador. You shall marry the Governor-General of India or the Lord-Lieutenant of Ireland, or somebody who wants a deputy-queen. I'm not going to have my masterpiece thrown away on Freddy.

LIZA: You think I like you to say that. But I haven't forgot what you said a minute ago; and I won't be coaxed round as if I was a baby or a puppy. If I can't have kindness, I'll have independence.

HIGGINS: Independence? That's middle class blasphemy. We are all dependent on one another, every soul of us on earth.

LIZA: [rising determinedly] I'll let you see whether I'm dependent on you. If you can preach, I can teach. I'll go and be a teacher.

HIGGINS: What'll you teach, in heaven's name?

LIZA: What you taught me. I'll teach phonetics.

HIGGINS: Ha! Ha! Ha!

LIZA: I'll offer myself as an assistant to Professor Nepean.

HIGGINS: [rising in a fury] What! That impostor! that humbug! that toadying ignoramus! Teach him my methods! my discoveries! You take one step in his direction and I'll wring your neck. [He lays hands on her]. Do you hear?

LIZA: [defiantly non-resistant] Wring away. What do I care? I knew you'd strike me some day. [He lets her go, stamping with rage at having forgotten himself, and recoils so hastily that he stumbles back into his seat on the ottoman]. Aha! Now I know how to deal with you. What a fool I was not to think of it before! You can't take away the knowledge you gave me. You said I had a finer ear than you. And I can be civil and kind to people, which is more than you can. Aha! That's done you, Henry Higgins, it has. Now I don't care that [snapping her fingers] for your bullying and your big talk. I'll advertize it in the papers that your duchess is only a flower girl that you taught, and that she'll teach anybody to be a duchess just the same in six months for a thousand guineas. Oh, when I think of myself crawling under your feet and being trampled on and called names, when all the time I had only to lift up my finger to be as good as you, I could just kick myself.

HIGGINS: [wondering at her] You damned impudent slut, you! But it's better than snivelling; better than fetching slippers and finding spectacles, isn't it? [Rising] By George, Eliza, I said I'd make a woman of you; and I have. I like you like this.

LIZA: Yes: you turn round and make up to me now that I'm not afraid of you, and can do without you.

HIGGINS: Of course I do, you little fool. Five minutes ago you were like a millstone round my neck. Now you're a tower of strength: a consort battleship. You and I and Pickering will be three old bachelors together instead of only two men and a silly girl.

[Mrs. Higgins returns, dressed for the wedding. Eliza instantly becomes cool and elegant.]

MRS. HIGGINS: The carriage is waiting, Eliza. Are you ready?

LIZA: Quite. Is the Professor coming?

MRS. HIGGINS: Certainly not. He can't behave himself in church. He makes remarks out loud all the time on the clergyman's pronunciation.

LIZA: Then I shall not see you again, Professor. Good bye. *[She goes to the door].*

MRS. HIGGINS: *[coming to Higgins]* Good-bye, dear.

HIGGINS: Good-bye, mother. *[He is about to kiss her, when he recollects something].* Oh, by the way, Eliza, order a ham and a Stilton cheese, will you? And buy me a pair of reindeer gloves, number eights, and a tie to match that new suit of mine, at Eale & Binman's. You can choose the color. *[His cheerful, careless, vigorous voice shows that he is incorrigible].*

LIZA: *[disdainfully]* Buy them yourself. *[She sweeps out].*

MRS. HIGGINS: I'm afraid you've spoiled that girl, Henry. But never mind, dear: I'll buy you the tie and gloves.

HIGGINS: *[sunnily]* Oh, don't bother. She'll buy em all right enough. Good-bye.

[They kiss. Mrs. Higgins runs out. Higgins, left alone, rattles his cash in his pocket; chuckles; and disports himself in a highly self-satisfied manner.]

****

The rest of the story need not be shown in action, and indeed, would hardly need telling if our imaginations were not so enfeebled by their lazy dependence on the ready-mades and reach-me-downs of the ragshop in which Romance keeps its stock of "happy endings" to misfit all stories. Now, the history of Eliza Doolittle, though called a romance because of the transfiguration it records seems exceedingly improbable, is common enough. Such transfigurations have been achieved by hundreds of resolutely ambitious young women since Nell Gwynne[†] set them the example by playing queens and fascinating kings in the theatre in which she began by selling oranges. Nevertheless, people in all directions have assumed, for no other reason than that she became the heroine of a romance, that she must have married the hero of it. This is unbearable, not only because her little drama, if acted on such a thoughtless assumption, must be spoiled, but because the true sequel is patent to anyone with a sense of human nature in general, and of feminine instinct in particular.

Eliza, in telling Higgins she would not marry him if he asked her, was not coquetting: she was announcing a well-considered decision. When a bachelor interests, and dominates, and teaches, and becomes important to a spinster, as Higgins with Eliza, she always, if she has character enough to be capable of it, considers very seriously indeed whether she will play for becoming that bachelor's wife, especially if he is so little interested in marriage that a determined and devoted woman might capture him if she set herself resolutely to do it. Her decision will depend a good deal on whether she is really free to choose; and that, again, will depend on her age and income. If she is at the end of her youth, and has no security for her livelihood, she will marry him because she must marry anybody who will provide for her. But at Eliza's age a good-looking girl does not feel that pressure; she feels free to pick and choose. She is therefore guided by her instinct in the matter. Eliza's instinct tells her not to marry Higgins. It does not tell her to give him up. It is not in the slightest doubt as to his remaining one of the strongest personal interests in her life. It would be very sorely strained if there was another woman likely to supplant her with him. But as she feels sure of him on that last point, she has no doubt at all as to her course, and would not have any, even if the difference of twenty years in age, which seems so great to youth, did not exist between them.

As our own instincts are not appealed to by her conclusion, let us see whether we cannot discover some reason in it. When Higgins excused his indifference to young women on the ground that they had an irresistible rival in his mother, he gave the clue to his inveterate old-bachelordom. The case is uncommon only to the extent that remarkable mothers are uncommon. If an imaginative boy has a sufficiently rich mother who has intelligence, personal grace, dignity of character without harshness, and a cultivated sense of the best art of her time to enable her to make her house beautiful, she sets a standard for him against which very few women can struggle, besides effecting for him a disengagement of his affections, his sense of beauty, and his idealism from his specifically sexual impulses. This makes him a standing puzzle to the huge number of uncultivated people who have been brought up in tasteless homes by commonplace or disagreeable parents, and to whom, consequently, literature, painting, sculpture, music, and affectionate personal relations come as modes of sex if they come at all. The word passion means nothing else to them; and that Higgins could have a passion for phonetics and idealize his mother instead of Eliza, would seem to them absurd and unnatural. Nevertheless, when we look round and see that hardly anyone is too ugly or disagreeable to find a wife or a husband if he or she wants one, whilst many old maids and bachelors are above the average in quality and culture, we cannot help suspecting that the disentanglement of sex from the associations with which it is so commonly confused, a disentanglement which persons of genius achieve by sheer intellectual analysis, is sometimes produced or aided by parental fascination.

Now, though Eliza was incapable of thus explaining to herself Higgins's formidable powers of resistance to the charm that prostrated Freddy at the first glance, she was instinctively aware that she could never obtain a complete grip of him, or come between him and his mother (the first necessity of the married woman). To put it shortly, she knew that for some mysterious reason he had not the makings of a married man in him, according to her conception of a husband as one to whom she would be his nearest and fondest and warmest interest. Even had there been no mother-rival, she would still have refused to accept an interest in herself that was secondary to philosophic interests. Had Mrs. Higgins died, there would still have been Milton and the Universal Alphabet. Landor's remark that to those who have the greatest power of loving, love is a secondary affair, would not have recommended Landor to Eliza. Put that along with her resentment of Higgins's domineering superiority, and her mistrust of his coaxing cleverness in getting round her and evading her wrath when he had gone too far with his impetuous bullying, and you will see that Eliza's instinct had good grounds for warning her not to marry her Pygmalion.

And now, whom did Eliza marry? For if Higgins was a predestinate old bachelor, she was most certainly not a predestinate old maid. Well, that can be told very shortly to those who have not guessed it from the indications she has herself given them.

Almost immediately after Eliza is stung into proclaiming her considered determination not to marry Higgins, she mentions the fact that young Mr. Frederick Eynsford Hill is pouring out his love for her daily through the post. Now Freddy is young, practically twenty years younger than Higgins: he is a gentleman (or, as Eliza would qualify him, a toff), and speaks like one; he is nicely dressed, is treated by the Colonel as an equal, loves her unaffectedly, and is not her master, nor ever likely to dominate her in spite of his advantage of social standing. Eliza has no use for the foolish romantic tradition that all women love to be mastered, if not actually bullied and beaten. "When you go to women," says Nietzsche,[†] "take your whip with you." Sensible despots have never confined that precaution to women: they have taken their whips with them when they have dealt with men, and been slavishly idealized by the men over whom they have flourished the whip much more than by women. No doubt there are slavish women as well as slavish men; and women, like men, admire those that are stronger than themselves. But to admire a strong person and to live under that strong person's thumb are two different things. The weak may not be admired and hero-worshipped; but they are by no means disliked or shunned; and they never seem to have the least difficulty in marrying people who are too good for them. They may fail in emergencies; but life is not one long emergency: it is mostly a string of situations for which no exceptional strength is needed, and with which even rather weak people can cope if they have a stronger partner to help them out. Accordingly, it is a truth everywhere in evidence that strong people, masculine or feminine, not only do not marry stronger people, but do not show any preference for them in selecting their friends. When a lion meets another with a louder roar "the first lion thinks the last a bore." The man or woman who feels strong enough for two, seeks for every other quality in a partner than strength.

The converse is also true. Weak people want to marry strong people who do not frighten them too much; and this often leads them to make the mistake we describe metaphorically as "biting off more than they can chew." They want too much for too little; and when the bargain is unreasonable beyond all bearing, the union becomes impossible: it ends in the weaker party being either discarded or borne as a cross, which is worse. People who are not only weak, but silly or obtuse as well, are often in these difficulties.

This being the state of human affairs, what is Eliza fairly sure to do when she is placed between Freddy and Higgins? Will she look forward to a lifetime of fetching Higgins's slippers or to a lifetime of Freddy fetching hers? There can be no doubt about the answer. Unless Freddy is biologically repulsive to her, and Higgins biologically attractive to a degree that overwhelms all her other instincts, she will, if she marries either of them, marry Freddy.

And that is just what Eliza did.

Complications ensued; but they were economic, not romantic. Freddy had no money and no occupation. His mother's jointure, a last relic of the opulence of Largelady Park, had enabled her to struggle along in Earlscourt with an air of gentility, but not to procure any serious secondary education for her children, much less give the boy a profession. A clerkship at thirty shillings a week was beneath Freddy's dignity, and extremely distasteful to him besides. His prospects consisted of a hope that if he kept up appearances somebody would do something for him. The something appeared vaguely to his imagination as a private secretaryship or a sinecure of some sort. To his mother it perhaps appeared as a marriage to some lady of means who could not resist her boy's niceness. Fancy her feelings when he married a flower girl who had become declassee under extraordinary circumstances which were now notorious!

It is true that Eliza's situation did not seem wholly ineligible. Her father, though formerly a dustman, and now fantastically disclassed, had become extremely popular in the smartest society by a social talent which triumphed over every prejudice and every disadvantage. Rejected by the middle class, which he loathed, he had shot up at once into the highest circles by his wit, his dustmanship (which he carried like a banner), and his Nietzschean transcendence of good and evil. At intimate ducal dinners he sat on the right hand of the Duchess; and in country houses he smoked in the pantry and was made much of by the butler when he was not feeding in the dining-room and being consulted by cabinet ministers. But he found it almost as hard to do all this on four thousand a year as Mrs. Eynsford Hill to live in Earlscourt on an income so pitiably smaller that I have not the heart to disclose its exact figure. He absolutely refused to add the last straw to his burden by contributing to Eliza's support.

Thus Freddy and Eliza, now Mr. and Mrs. Eynsford Hill, would have spent a penniless honeymoon but for a wedding present £500 from the Colonel to Eliza. It lasted a long time because Freddy did not know how to spend money, never having had any to spend, and Eliza, socially trained by a pair of old bachelors, wore her clothes as long as they held together and looked pretty, without the least regard to their being many months out of fashion. Still, £500 will not last two young people for ever; and they both knew, and Eliza felt as well, that they must shift for themselves in the end. She could quarter herself on Wimpole Street because it had come to be her home; but she was quite aware that she ought not to quarter Freddy there, and that it would not be good for his character if she did.

Not that the Wimpole Street bachelors objected. When she consulted them, Higgins declined to be bothered about her housing problem when that solution was so simple. Eliza's desire to have Freddy in the house with her seemed of no more importance than if she had wanted an extra piece of bedroom furniture. Pleas as to Freddy's character, and the moral obligation on him to earn his own living, were lost on Higgins. He denied that Freddy had any character, and declared that if he tried to do any useful work some competent person would have the trouble of undoing it: a procedure involving a net loss to the community, and great unhappiness to Freddy himself, who was obviously intended by Nature for such light work as amusing Eliza, which, Higgins declared, was a much more useful and honorable occupation than working in the city. When Eliza referred again to her project of teaching phonetics, Higgins abated not a jot of his violent opposition to it. He said she was not within ten years of being qualified to meddle with his pet subject; and as it was evident that the Colonel agreed with him, she felt she could not go against them in this grave matter, and that she had no right, without Higgins's consent, to exploit the knowledge he had given her; for his knowledge seemed to her as much his private property as his watch: Eliza was no communist. Besides, she was superstitiously devoted to them both, more entirely and frankly after her marriage than before it.

It was the Colonel who finally solved the problem, which had cost him much perplexed cogitation. He one day asked Eliza, rather shyly, whether she had quite given up her notion of keeping a flower shop. She replied that she had thought of it, but had put it out of her head, because the Colonel had said, that day at Mrs. Higgins's, that it would never do. The Colonel confessed that when he said that, he had not quite recovered from the dazzling impression of the day before. They broke the matter to Higgins that evening. The sole comment vouchsafed by him very nearly led to a serious quarrel with Eliza. It was to the effect that she would have in Freddy an ideal errand boy.

Freddy himself was next sounded on the subject. He said he had been thinking of a shop himself; though it had presented itself to his pennilessness as a small place in which Eliza should sell tobacco at one counter whilst he sold newspapers at the opposite one. But he agreed that it would be extraordinarily jolly to go early every morning with Eliza to Covent Garden and buy flowers on the scene of their first meeting: a sentiment which earned him many kisses from his wife. He added that he had always been afraid to propose anything of the sort, because Clara would make an awful row about a step that must damage her matrimonial chances, and his mother could not be expected to like it after clinging for so many years to that step of the social ladder on which retail trade is impossible.

This difficulty was removed by an event highly unexpected by Freddy's mother. Clara, in the course of her incursions into those artistic circles which were the highest within her reach, discovered that her conversational qualifications were expected to include a grounding in the novels of Mr. H.G. Wells.[†] She borrowed them in various directions so energetically that she swallowed them all within two months. The result was a conversion of a kind quite common today. A modern Acts of the Apostles would fill fifty whole Bibles if anyone were capable of writing it.

Poor Clara, who appeared to Higgins and his mother as a disagreeable and ridiculous person, and to her own mother as in some inexplicable way a social failure, had never seen herself in either light; for, though to some extent ridiculed and mimicked in West Kensington like everybody else there, she was accepted as a rational and normal—or shall we say inevitable?—sort of human being. At worst they called her The Pusher; but to them no more than to herself had it ever occurred that she was pushing the air, and pushing it in a wrong direction. Still, she was not happy. She was growing desperate. Her one asset, the fact that her mother was what the Epsom greengrocer called a carriage lady had no exchange value, apparently. It had prevented her from getting educated, because the only education she could have afforded was education with the Earlscourt green grocer's daughter. It had led her to seek the society of her mother's class; and that class simply would not have her, because she was much poorer than the greengrocer, and, far from being able to afford a maid, could not afford even a housemaid, and had to scrape along at home with an illiberally treated general servant. Under such circumstances nothing could give her an air of being a genuine product of Largelady Park. And yet its tradition made her regard a marriage with anyone within her reach as an unbearable humiliation. Commercial people and professional people in a small way were odious to her. She ran after painters and novelists; but she did not charm them; and her bold attempts to pick up and practise artistic and literary talk irritated them. She was, in short, an utter failure, an ignorant, incompetent, pretentious, unwelcome, penniless, useless little snob; and though she did not admit these disqualifications (for nobody ever faces unpleasant truths of this kind until the possibility of a way out dawns on them) she felt their effects too keenly to be satisfied with her position.

Clara had a startling eyeopener when, on being suddenly wakened to enthusiasm by a girl of her own age who dazzled her and produced in her a gushing desire to take her for a model, and gain her friendship, she discovered that this exquisite apparition had graduated from the gutter in a few months' time. It shook her so violently, that when Mr. H. G. Wells lifted her on the point of his puissant pen, and placed her at the angle of view from which the life she was leading and the society to which she clung appeared in its true relation to real human needs and worthy social structure, he effected a conversion and a conviction of sin comparable to the most sensational feats of General Booth[†] or Gypsy Smith.[†] Clara's snobbery went bang. Life suddenly began to move with her. Without knowing how or why, she began to make friends and enemies. Some of the acquaintances to whom she had been a tedious or indifferent or ridiculous affliction, dropped her: others became cordial. To her amazement she found that some "quite nice" people were saturated with Wells, and that this accessibility to ideas was the secret of their niceness. People she had thought deeply religious, and had tried to conciliate on that tack with disastrous results, suddenly took an interest in her, and revealed a hostility to conventional religion which she had never conceived possible except among the most desperate characters. They made her read Galsworthy; and Galsworthy exposed the vanity of Largelady Park and finished her. It exasperated her to think that the dungeon in which she had languished for so many unhappy years had been unlocked all the time, and that the impulses she had so carefully struggled with and stifled for the sake of keeping well with society, were precisely those by which alone she could have come into any sort of sincere human contact. In the radiance of these discoveries, and the tumult of their reaction, she made a fool of herself as freely and conspicuously as when she so rashly adopted Eliza's expletive in Mrs. Higgins's drawing-room; for the new-born Wellsian had to find her bearings almost as ridiculously as a baby; but nobody hates a baby for its ineptitudes, or thinks the worse of it for trying to eat the matches; and Clara lost no friends by her follies. They laughed at her to her face this time; and she had to defend herself and fight it out as best she could.

When Freddy paid a visit to Earlscourt (which he never did when he could possibly help it) to make the desolating announcement that he and his Eliza were thinking of blackening the Largelady scutcheon by opening a shop, he found the little household already convulsed by a prior announcement from Clara that she also was going to work in an old furniture shop in Dover Street, which had been started by a fellow Wellsian. This appointment Clara owed, after all, to her old social accomplishment of Push. She had made up her mind that, cost what it might, she would see Mr. Wells in the flesh; and she had achieved her end at a garden party. She had better luck than so rash an enterprise deserved. Mr. Wells came up to her expectations. Age had not withered him, nor could custom stale his infinite variety in half an hour. His pleasant neatness and compactness, his small hands and feet, his teeming ready brain, his unaffected accessibility, and a certain fine apprehensiveness which stamped him as susceptible from his topmost hair to his tipmost toe, proved irresistible. Clara talked of nothing else for weeks and weeks afterwards. And as she happened to talk to the lady of the furniture shop, and that lady also desired above all things to know Mr. Wells and sell pretty things to him, she offered Clara a job on the chance of achieving that end through her.

And so it came about that Eliza's luck held, and the expected opposition to the flower shop melted away. The shop is in the arcade of a railway station not very far from the Victoria and Albert Museum; and if you live in that neighborhood you may go there any day and buy a buttonhole from Eliza.

Now here is a last opportunity for romance. Would you not like to be assured that the shop was an immense success, thanks to Eliza's charms and her early business experience in Covent Garden? Alas! the truth is the truth: the shop did not pay for a long time, simply because Eliza and her Freddy did not know how to keep it. True, Eliza had not to begin at the very beginning: she knew the names and prices of the cheaper flowers; and her elation was unbounded when she found that Freddy, like all youths educated at cheap, pretentious, and thoroughly inefficient schools, knew a little Latin. It was very little, but enough to make him appear to her a Porson or Bentley, and to put him at his ease with botanical nomenclature. Unfortunately he knew nothing else; and Eliza, though she could count money up to eighteen shillings or so, and had acquired a certain familiarity with the language of Milton from her struggles to qualify herself for winning Higgins's bet, could not write out a bill without utterly disgracing the establishment. Freddy's power of stating in Latin that Balbus built a wall and that Gaul was divided into three parts did not carry with it the slightest knowledge of accounts or business: Colonel Pickering had to explain to him what a cheque book and a bank account meant. And the pair were by no means easily teachable. Freddy backed up Eliza in her obstinate refusal to believe that they could save money by engaging a bookkeeper with some knowledge of the business. How, they argued, could you possibly save money by going to extra expense when you already could not make both ends meet? But the Colonel, after making the ends meet over and over again, at last gently insisted; and Eliza, humbled to the dust by having to beg from him so often, and stung by the uproarious derision of Higgins, to whom the notion of Freddy succeeding at anything was a joke that never palled, grasped the fact that business, like phonetics, has to be learned.

On the piteous spectacle of the pair spending their evenings in shorthand schools and polytechnic classes, learning bookkeeping and typewriting with incipient junior clerks, male and female, from the elementary schools, let me not dwell. There were even classes at the London School of Economics, and a humble personal appeal to the director of that institution to recommend a course bearing on the flower business. He, being a humorist, explained to them the method of the celebrated Dickensian essay on Chinese Metaphysics by the gentleman who read an article on China and an article on Metaphysics and combined the information. He suggested that they should combine the London School with Kew Gardens. Eliza, to whom the procedure of the Dickensian gentleman seemed perfectly correct (as in fact it was) and not in the least funny (which was only her ignorance) took his advice with entire gravity. But the effort that cost her the deepest humiliation was a request to Higgins, whose pet artistic fancy, next to Milton's verse, was calligraphy, and who himself wrote a most beautiful Italian hand, that he would teach her to write. He declared that she was congenitally incapable of forming a single letter worthy of the least of Milton's words; but she persisted; and again he suddenly threw himself into the task of teaching her with a combination of stormy intensity, concentrated patience, and occasional bursts of interesting disquisition on the beauty and nobility, the august mission and destiny, of human handwriting. Eliza ended by acquiring an extremely uncommercial script which was a positive extension of her personal beauty, and spending three times as much on stationery as anyone else because certain qualities and shapes of paper became indispensable to her. She could not even address an envelope in the usual way because it made the margins all wrong.

Their commercial school days were a period of disgrace and despair for the young couple. They seemed to be learning nothing about flower shops. At last they gave it up as hopeless, and shook the dust of the shorthand schools, and the polytechnics, and the London School of Economics from their feet for ever. Besides, the business was in some mysterious way beginning to take care of itself. They had somehow forgotten their objections to employing other people. They came to the conclusion that their own way was the best, and that they had really a remarkable talent for business. The Colonel, who had been compelled for some years to keep a sufficient sum on current account at his bankers to make up their deficits, found that the provision was unnecessary: the young people were prospering. It is true that there was not quite fair play between them and their competitors in trade. Their week-ends in the country cost them nothing, and saved them the price of their Sunday dinners; for the motor car was the Colonel's; and he and Higgins paid the hotel bills. Mr. F. Hill, florist and greengrocer (they soon discovered that there was money in asparagus; and asparagus led to other vegetables), had an air which stamped the business as classy; and in private life he was still Frederick Eynsford Hill, Esquire. Not that there was any swank about him: nobody but Eliza knew that he had been christened Frederick Challoner. Eliza herself swanked like anything.

That is all. That is how it has turned out. It is astonishing how much Eliza still manages to meddle in the housekeeping at Wimpole Street in spite of the shop and her own family. And it is notable that though she never nags her husband, and frankly loves the Colonel as if she were his favorite daughter, she has never got out of the habit of nagging Higgins that was established on the fatal night when she won his bet for him. She snaps his head off on the faintest provocation, or on none. He no longer dares to tease her by assuming an abysmal inferiority of Freddy's mind to his own. He storms and bullies and derides; but she stands up to him so ruthlessly that the Colonel has to ask her from time to time to be kinder to Higgins; and it is the only request of his that brings a mulish expression into her face. Nothing but some emergency or calamity great enough to break down all likes and dislikes, and throw them both back on their common humanity—and may they be spared any such trial!—will ever alter this. She knows that Higgins does not need her, just as her father did not need her. The very scrupulousness with which he told her that day that he had become used to having her there, and dependent on her for all sorts of little services, and that he should miss her if she went away (it would never have occurred to Freddy or the Colonel to say anything of the sort) deepens her inner certainty that she is "no more to him than them slippers", yet she has a sense, too, that his indifference is deeper than the infatuation of commoner souls. She is immensely interested in him. She has even secret mischievous moments in which she wishes she could get him alone, on a desert island, away from all ties and with nobody else in the world to consider, and just drag him off his pedestal and see him making love like any common man. We all have private imaginations of that sort. But when it comes to business, to the life that she really leads as distinguished from the life of dreams and fancies, she likes Freddy and she likes the Colonel; and she does not like Higgins and Mr. Doolittle. Galatea never does quite like Pygmalion: his relation to her is too godlike to be altogether agreeable.

GLOSSARY

Preface

Melville Bell – (1819–1905) a Scottish American teacher who wrote about education and the science of speech; he created an alphabet with symbols that represented every sound of the human voice. Bell was the father of Alexander Graham Bell.

Alexander J. Ellis – (1814-1890) an English scholar of linguistics

Henry Sweet – (1845-1912) the founder of modern phonetics; sweet was a British phonetician and scholar of linguistics. He is well known for his *History of English Sounds.*

Ibsen – Henrik Ibsen (1828-1906) is known as the "father of modern drama." The Norwegian playwright is known for his psychological dramas and commentaries on social issues of the day. His plays are still frequently performed globally.

Samuel Butler – (1835-1902) a British writer; he is best known for *The Way of All Flesh*, a satire on family life in mid-Victorian England.

Imperial Institute – built as the National memorial of Queen Victoria's Jubilee in the United Kingdom (1887-1893); the Institute's objective was to spread knowledge of agriculture, commerce, and industrial progress throughout the Empire.

Joseph Chamberlain – (1836-1914) a British statesman who advocated radical social reform throughout his political career

Oxford – one of the oldest English-language universities in the world; built in the 12th century in England, it was the center of learning throughout the Middle Ages. Oxford University still maintains an outstanding reputation for its academic programs.

Pitman System of Shorthand – a phonetic system of rapid writing developed by Sir Isaac Pitman, first presented in 1837

Sybil – This is a reference to "Spelt from Sybil's Leaves," a poem written by Gerard Manley Hopkins. The poem discusses the consequences that occur when opposites (such as good and evil) are not resolved.

The Times – a daily newspaper in the United Kingdom; it is called the *London Times* by those living outside of Britain.

"…Thersites railed at Ajax…" – In Greek mythology, Thersites was a soldier in the Greek army during the Trojan War. Thersites also appears in Shakespeare's play *The History of Troilus and Cressida* in which he is Ajax's slave.

Pygmalion – According to Greek mythology, a king of Cyprus carved a statue of a woman and fell in love with it. Aphrodite, the goddess of love, brought the statue to life as Galatea. Note the similarities between the myth and the play, although the play does not attempt to accurately portray the events in the myth.

Thames – a major river in England

Poet Laureate – a poet appointed by a British monarch to be a member of the royal household for life; the poet was expected to write about celebrated occasions and to honor the royal family.

Miltonic – pertaining to the English poet John Milton (1608-1674); he is best known for *Paradise Lost*, an epic poem about humanity's fall from grace.

Academy of Dramatic Art – a British stage school established in 1904 by Sir Herbert Beerbohm Tree, a Shakespearean producer

Act I

Spoken Sanscrit [sic] – Sanskrit is India's classical, ancient literary language

"have a jaw over" – to have a discussion

"his Pharisaic want of charity" – This phrase means hypocritically self-righteous. Higgins's desire to help Liza is self-serving, since he uses her speech to further his own work.

Act II

Piranesis – Giovanni Battista Piranesi (1720-1778) was an Italian architect and artist who created etchings of Rome and its ruins.

mezzotint portraits – copper or steel plate engravings

Buckingham Palace – Built in 1703, Buckingham Palace is the residence of British kings and queens in London, England.

Tower of London – an ancient fortress in London, England, near the River Thames that has been used as a royal residence and a jail for prisoners; the Traitors' Gate and the Bloody Tower of the fortress are associated with many prominent historical figures.

"...seat in the Cabinet and a popular pulpit in Wales." – The cabinet is a group appointed by the Prime Minister of England that acts as official advisor. A "pulpit" represents a position as a preacher. Wales is a principality of Britain, but has kept its own culture. Higgins and Pickering, here, believe they can raise Doolittle's status to become a prominent figure since they have elevated Liza.

Act III

"...Morris wall-papers, and the Morris chintz window curtains..." – items from the famous designer William Morris (1834-1896), a British poet, painter, craftsman, and social reformer; he is best known for his wallpaper and furniture designs.

Grosvenor Gallery – founded in London (1877) for displaying independent exhibitions of established painters and sculptors

Burne Jones – (1833-1898) He was a British painter and member of the Pre-Raphaelite Brotherhood, a society that advanced Italian painting style before Raphael. Burne-Jones is known both for having a mystical, dreamlike style in his paintings and for stained-glass designs.

Whistler – James Abbott McNeill Whistler (1834-1903) was one of the best-known painters in the later half of the 1800s. He specialized in landscapes and portraits.

Cecil Lawson – (1851-1882) an English landscape painter

"...on the scale of a Rubens." – Peter Paul Rubens (1577-1640) was famous in the art world during the 17th-century in Spain, Italy, France, and England and is still considered one of the most important artists in history.

Chippendale chair – of the style of Thomas Chippendale, a furniture maker in the 18th century. Pieces of furniture are described as "Chippendale" if they feature elaborate hand carvings in his styles.

Inigo Jones – (1573-1652) an English architect; he designed the Queen's House in Greenwich, England, and the Banqueting Hall in Whitehall, London.

Royal Society's soirees – parties held by the oldest scientific organization in Great Britain; the Royal Society was founded by a group of men in London to promote scientific discussion in 1660.

a ship's forecastle – the front section of a boat, traditonally the location of the crew's living quarters

Hyde Park – a public park in London

"...Beethoven and Brahms or Lehar and Lionel Morickton..." – famous musical composers

Act IV

—

Act V

Moral Reform Societies – These organizations were formed by people who wanted to change societal beliefs and behaviors with regard to such issues as drunkenness, slavery, and sexuality. Societies were formed with varying members of classes, races, and genders.

Nell Gwynne – Eleanor Gwyn (1650-1687) was an English actress known for her comic roles in theatre and interpretations of prologues and epilogues. She was an orange-seller at the Theatre Royal who became a member of Thomas Killigrew's theatre company.

Nietzsche – Friedrich Wilhelm Nietzsche (1844-1900) was a German philosopher who rejected bourgeois civilization and Christianity. The philosopher put forth the concept of a "superman" ("ubermensch" in German), who represented a level of morality that went beyond conventional ideas of good and evil.

H.G. Wells – (1866-1946) an English author who is best known for his science fiction novels

General Booth – William Booth (1829-1912) was an English religious leader and founder of the Salvation Army. He started the Christian Mission, which became the Salvation Army in 1878, with his wife, Catherine Booth.

Gypsy Smith – Rodney Smith (1860-1947) was a British evangelist. He was born into a gypsy family and received no education. Smith joined William Booth's mission and conducted religious campaigns in the United States and Scotland for more than seventy years. Large crowds would gather to hear his messages.

VOCABULARY

Preface

amenity – pleasantness, attractiveness
aspirant – someone who seeks a high position or advancement
conciliatory – appeasing, pacifying, reconciling
cryptograms – coded or secret writings
decipher – to interpret, decode
derisive – mocking; sarcastic
didactic – morally instructive
eminence – a position of superiority
exorbitant – excessive
inscrutable – difficult to understand; mysterious
libelous – defamatory; slanderous
repudiation – refusing to honor something previously agreed to
satires – literary works that use humor to ridicule something or someone
syndicate – a business that sells publications to periodicals
vulgarly – crudely, offensively

Act I

bilious – ill-humored
brogue – an accent
crooning – singing, humming softly
detestable – abominable; despicable; loathsome; repugnant
draught – a current of air
genially – graciously
grandeur – nobility of character, magnificence
gumption – boldness; aggressiveness
half-a-crown – a silver coin worth 2.5 shillings
half-sovereign – a gold coin worth 10 shillings
impertinent – improperly forward or bold
mendacity – untruthfulness
pence – the plural form for a penny
plinth – the supporting block or slab of a column
portico – a roofed porch or walkway supported by columns
rebuking – reprimanding; criticizing sharply

toff – [slang] a member of the upper class
uproariously – boisterously

Act II

audacity – boldness, nerve
balmies – [slang] people with eccentric behaviors
benzine – a flammable liquid
callous – unfeeling; emotionally hardened
conceited – vain; self-absorbed
dainty – delicately beautiful; charming
deplorable – wretched; woeful
exquisitely – beautifully; flawlessly
farthing – a coin worth one-quarter of a penny
genteel – well-bred; polite; refined
guineas – gold coins
incensed – infuriated
jaunt – a short trip or outing
laryngoscope – a tube used to examine the vocal cords
magisterially – in a dignified manner
navvy – [slang] a laborer
pathos – a quality that arouses sympathy or pity
pauperize – to impoverish
petulance – irritability, peevishness
phonograph – a record player
prudery – excessive modesty
remonstrance – a complaint
rhetoric – the art of using language persuasively and effectively
slovenly – untidy; sloppy
wallop – to beat, thrash
zephyr – a wind current

Act III

"Ahdedo" – [dialect] "How do you do?"
barometrical – relating to atmospheric pressure
brusquely – discourteously blunt

caricatured – misrepresented
compulsory – obligatory; required
diphtheria – an infectious disease
discontentedly – unhappily
divan – a backless sofa
estheticism – a refined taste
extricating – releasing from difficulty; disengaging
gramophone disks – records for a phonograph
pedantic – academic; scholastic; overly preachy
pretension – a showy display
rotters – [slang] scoundrels
sanguinary – bloody
settee – a medium-sized sofa

Act IV

billet-doux – a love letter
condescending – patronizing; displaying a superior attitude
dudgeon – angry humor
fervently – emotionally; strongly
indifferent – not caring either way; apathetic
pantomime – communication through gestures and facial expressions
    without words
perfunctorily – carelessly; with little interest
presumptuous – excessively forward
purgatory – suffering
shied – threw, flung
superlatively – outstandingly, greatly
tomfoollery – [**tomfoolery**] foolish behavior

Act V

abated – lessened; decreased
abysmal – limitless; unfathomable
accosts – approaches aggressively
bequest – a gift
blighter – someone held in low esteem

botanical – relating to plants
coquetting – flirting
declassee – of inferior social status
demean – to debase; to degrade
illiberally – in a mean or stingy manner
impudence – offensively bold behavior
incorrigible – incapable of reform
inveterate – deeply rooted; habitual
magnanimous – forgiving; unselfish
malice – ill will, spite
nomenclature – the assigning of names and categories to organisms
odious – hateful
opulence – wealth
perplexed – confused; bewildered
predestinate – determined in advance
proffered – offered for acceptance
prostrated – caused to fall down
Providence – God
repudiate – to reject or refuse
rogue – a scoundrel or rascal
snivelling – [**sniveling**] complaining, whining
swank – pretentious or ostentatious behavior
teeming – full of things
toadying – flattering others for self-serving reasons
tumult – a commotion or disturbance
vehement – intense
vexed – annoyed; distressed; irritated
vouchsafed – granted in a condescending way

Insightful and Reader-Friendly, Yet Affordable

Prestwick House Literary Touchstone Classic Editions–
The Editions By Which All Others May Be Judged

Every *Prestwick House Literary Touchstone Classic* is enhanced with Reading Pointers for Sharper Insight to improve comprehension and provide insights that will help students recognize key themes, symbols, and plot complexities. In addition, each title includes a Glossary of the more difficult words and concepts.

For the Shakespeare titles, along with the Reading Pointers and Glossary, we include margin notes and various strategies to understanding the language of Shakespeare.

New titles are constantly being added; call or visit our website for current listing.

Special Educator's Discount – At Least

50% Off